Maria Moss

We've Been Here Before

Nordamerika-Studien
North American Studies

herausgegeben von

Norbert Finzsch und Rolf Meyn
Universität Hamburg

Band 1

LIT

Maria Moss

We've Been Here Before

Women in Creation Myths and Contemporary Literature of the Native American Southwest

LIT

gedruckt mit Unterstützung der Universität Hamburg

Die Deutsche Bibliothek – CIP-Einheitsaufnahme

Moss, Maria
We've Been Here Before
: Women in Creation Myths and Contemporary Literature of the Native American Southwest / Maria Moss . – Münster ; Hamburg : Lit 1993
(Nordamerika-Studien; Bd. 1.)
ISBN 3-89473-928-2

NE: GT

Dieckstraße 56 48145 Münster Tel. 0251-235091
Hallerplatz 5 20146 Hamburg Tel. 040-446446

WE'VE BEEN HERE BEFORE

* * *

Women in Creation Myths

and

Contemporary Literature

of the

Native American Southwest

Say this: say in my mind

I saw your spiders weaving threads
to bandage up the day. And more,
those webs were filled with words
that tumbled meaning into wind.

James Welch
"Snow Country Weavers"[1]

This Ph.D. project is strongly influenced by the canon discussion that has been keeping critics, teachers, and lovers of literature busy worrying about the processes that are currently challenging the existing canon in the United States. It is both an attempt to demonstrate what David Harvey called "an openness to an unassimilated otherness,"[2] and a contribution to the dialogue with the "Other", that is, "the subjects that have historically formed the boundaries of [our] cultural experiences."[3]

When I first decided to write my dissertation on Native American literature I did not realize that different philosophical and literary concepts may warrant different modes of interpretation. Eventually, however, a question posed itself: could I examine a literature which takes its symbolic implication, its literary expression, and its structural framework from the oral tradition handed down through the centuries with the same literary tools that I had used for previous critical writings? Initially, my answer was a clear "yes." Once I delved deeper into the analysis of Native American literature, however, I realized that my mode of interpretation had to shift. Since significant aspects of native literature do not abide by the analytic laws of the cause and effect theory, causal connections merely led away from a more profound understanding of primal concepts. In order to do justice to the works explored it is necessary, as Lauter states, to suspend "our assumptions about formal hierarchy and concentrate on discovering the formal conventions that emerge from those literatures rather than from our training as literary practitioners."[4]

Regarding their novels as storytellers would regard their tales, all four novelists assume, or pretend to assume, that their audience is familiar with the traditions of oral accounts. Hence, they seldom introduce and never elaborate on the themes and symbols employed. This places the reader unfamiliar with Native American literature in a somewhat difficult, yet highly challenging, position. If s/he is unwilling to enter a world filled with incomprehensible myths, omnipresent supernaturals, and sacred symbols, the novels are bound to be viewed as children's folktales. In the event of an awakening interest on part of the reader, however, s/he cannot possibly escape the larger implications connected to the study of Native American literature. Different levels of consciousness will be activated in that case: the political, the mythological, the intuitive. Relative to the strenuous effort needed, the outcome will be rewarding.

The tools of myth criticism will be instrumental for the interpretation of the four novels. The structure, the meaning, and the overall significance of myth have also been researched by non-native scholars like Northrop Frye, Claude Lévi-Strauss, Ernst Cassirer, and Hans Blumenberg. Their findings concerning the functional multitude of mythic structures greatly facilitated the initial understanding of the works under consideration. Like the literature to be discussed below, myth criticism is based on and takes into account the themes and structures of mythology. Since the devices of myth criticism will be employed to discover meaning, it is of utmost importance to abandon causal concepts and psychological evaluations. In order to follow the novels' web-like structure which reflects the interrelatedness of the tribes' universe, the mind has to follow criss-cross references while thinking in analogies in order to comprehend the overall significance of native literature and proceed to its center of meaning.

As a consequence of a nonlinear, nonsequential set of correspondences, my interpretation could not proceed from A to Z in a linear manner, but had to circle around the central issue, not like a cat around the hot milk never daring to approach it, but like a critic abiding by the cyclical nature of the novels with an interpretation that would do justice to the philosophical ideas brought forth. I could not use the printed, mostly lyrical, version of the origin stories as a blueprint to draw analogies for an interpretation of Native American novels without adhering, at least in part, to the basic structure of both the traditional myths and the contemporary literature based on those myths. This is not to say that the arguments are not clear, sound, or well-explained. But that is for the reader to decide.

I would like to say "thank you" to Prof. Dr. Rolf Meyn for his willingness to be my "Doktorvater" and for his continued support in "times of trouble." I would also like to thank Prof. Schöpp for agreeing to be the co-reader. A "Dankeschön" to my parents whose generous support greatly facilitated the writing of this dissertation. Last, but not least, I am indebted to three people who were there when despair seemed to be looming just around the corner: to Martin and his readiness and patience to over and over again discuss different philosophical concepts, to Ingo whose translating abilities came in handy at a time when the world seemed to collapse, and to Claus who made the computer understand what I had to say.

CONTENTS

I. Introduction

The purpose of this dissertation is to explore the role of women in four of the best-known and most outstanding Native American novels of the past two decades. In that context I will trace the influence of the "female" back to the origin stories, or creation myths, of the American Southwest. I will emphasize the important role Native American women have played and continue to play as members of primeval cultures, both in a historical as well as in a mythological context. Prior to any discussion of the novels under consideration in the context of southwestern myths, I will familiarize the reader with the socio-historical and the philosophic-literary concepts of Native America. The ethnography of the Southwest will be emphasized.

A brief historical survey contains examples of the decline of woman-focused tribes and a) serves as an introduction to the larger historical context of Native America, b) gives an explanation for the desolate situation that exists at the outset of all four novels, and c) establishes the woman as culture-bearer in history, a role that mirrors her significance in mythology. Myths will be examined as sources not devoid of historical significance. It will become apparent that Lévi-Strauss' question, 'where does mythology end and history start?'[1] gains paramount importance in the context of an oral tradition which simultaneously functions as historical documentation. A philosophical overview is equally indispensable since the Native American approach to basic philosophical concepts differs greatly from western thought in its perception of reality, and consequently, in its assumption about literary creations. The tribes' origin myths and related chantways--both of which will be dealt with in detail--include examples of the most accomplished expressions of oral literature. Since written literature constitutes a fairly recent phenomenon in the literary history of Native America, and since both formal aspects organic to native literature as well as the majority of its stories and themes emerge from the structures and events of the oral tradition, a summary of the oral elements in written literature is essential. The oral tradition contains information regarding mythic events. These elements, however, will not be viewed as mere fantasies, but instead as constituting, initiating, or backing up historical facts. Altogether, chapters II and III will provide the reader with the background necessary to open "to new ways of observing and registering the world through Indian concepts of literature and language."[2]

Native American mythologies provide examples of primal religious traditions and social structures that have been present in North America for possibly up to forty-thousand years. Yet, ever-increasing contact with representatives of mostly European civilizations led to immense changes within tribal cultures since the late fifteenth century. "Under this impact," writes Joseph Epes Brown, "certain tribal groups and even linguistic families became extinct, while others became acculturated to varying degrees into the dominant societies."[3] Frequently, matrifocal tribal structures changed into European-style patriarchies due to the influence of the colonizers. In the American Southwest, however, elements fundamental to tribal traditions survive into the present and are currently being reaffirmed by native peoples and reexamined by native novelists.

The emphasis in this dissertation will be placed upon the present viability of mythic elements in contemporary literature. The mythological structures pertinent to the interpretation of native literature will not only be revealed, but also evaluated in terms of their significance for the behavior and development of the characters in contemporary literature. Since native literature is intimately tied to rituals and ceremonies which, in turn, are based on the creation myths, myth criticism serves as an adequate tool for the interpretation of native writing. Myth, like native ritual, "introduces us to a world where the inevitable movement from cause to effect, the inevitable separation of one thing from another thing, no longer exists."[4] Still, as Blumenberg points out in his influential work on mythology, Arbeit am Mythos, myths reveal their own distinct connectedness to reality. 'Relatedness to reality does not mean empirical proof', he maintains, 'but matter-of-factness, familiarity, an archaic feeling of belonging into the universe'.[5]

Myth criticism creates meaning through uncovering the correspondences--such as similarities, differences, synchronism, circularity, and simultaneity of specific events and structures--which coincidence alone cannot account for. The individual elements are often insubstantial and meaningless; regarded within a net of correspondences, however, the connection of different components creates meaning. Blumenberg maintains that myths are stories that feature a 'lasting and significant consistency of their narrative center and a similarly pronounced marginal variability'. ' Myths', he continues, are thus not »sacred« texts that cannot be changed even one iota'.[6] The "marginal variability" of mythic stories corresponds to the ever-changing accounts of oral literature and the fluctuating performances of rituals and ceremonies. Both exhibit a "range of acceptable variations, compromises between the idealized need to do things 'correctly' [and] reality." Within limits, there is "room for individual decision making, discussion, negotiation, and even creativity."[7]

The Native American novels to be discussed below are based on mythic stories from two cultures, the Navajos and the Pueblos of the American Southwest. Besides early modifications within the myths due to changing geographic conditions and/or their relative closeness to other myth cycles, the artists' creative restructuring of mythic tales as well as the incorporation of unrelated myths occur. To reduce mythic structures to one 'single and true' basic or original myth (if this could ever be achieved) would mean to view the modifications as structured or artificial. Of concern here are not the highly speculative questions regarding the original myth(s), but the mythic elements that have survived into the present, notwithstanding either their chronological or cultural origin or their revisions by the novelists. I will therefore follow Blumenberg's theory that any 'basic' myth consists of the ultimately, **not** the originally, existent myth. It is this resistance of mythic structures and elements, the 'firmness regarding the temporal processes of corrosion'[8] that constitutes the original myth.

The origin stories are held together by an elaborate system of symbolism in which, for instance, colors, direction, location, and animals possess numinous qualities. In order to counteract possible omnipotent powers, bearers of numinous aspects are not only people or mythic characters alone. This has very practical reasons: since geographical features are equipped with mythic significance, the stories, according to Silko "cannot be separated from geographical location." Since they are "so much a part of these places . . . it is almost impossible for future generations to lose the stories because there are so many imposing geological elements."[9] Not only their sense of belonging in an ancestral way, but their eventual acceptance of the land's mythic power plays an essential role in the characters' development towards physical and emotional integrity. Thus, place, the junction of geographical features and mythic significance, is not only an aspect of the novels--it may have made them possible.

Since written works based foremost on the symbolic implications of oral accounts are intimately tied to the mythic traditions and social structures of the group that produced them, each body of tribal literature must be studied within its cultural context. The novels under consideration have all been written by southwestern novelists and take place largely in Arizona and New Mexico; thus, they are inextricably linked to the mythologies, symbols, rituals, and oral traditions of the Southwest. The symbols cannot be understood in terms of another culture, writes Allen, "whether it be that of Maya or of England, because those other cultures have different imperatives and have grown on different soil, under a different sky within the nexus of different spirits, and within a different spiritual context."[10] To the extent that knowledge of Greek and Roman mythologies makes western cultures accessible to the understanding, the Pueblo and Navajo origin stories make southwestern literatures available for scholarly interpretation and research. To be unaware of the creation myths, the meaning of their symbols, and their accompanying ritualistic codes, is to miss part of the significance of contemporary native literature. "The events of creation," as Sam Gill points out, are "paradigmatic and the knowledge given in the creation stories permeates the life of the people."[11]

Since the mythopoeic imagination does not consider myth a symbolic expression of an independent reality but believes in the actual synonymity of symbol and object, mythical symbols--whether animated or not--are to be interpreted literally, not allegorically. A participant in ceremonies, for instance, "does not regard himself as engaging in mere imitative representation but as becoming identified momentarily with the person of the mythical drama and exercising his powers."[12]

Making significant contributions to contemporary Native American literature are a number of southwestern authors whose works have their roots in the oral tradition of their respective tribes. House Made Of Dawn (1968), Ceremony (1977), The Woman Who Owned The Shadows (1983), and The Ancient Child (1989), focus on important socio-political issues while simultaneously displaying significant aspects of Pueblo and Navajo mythology.[13] Excepting Allen's novel, women seem to play a secondary role to that of the male protagonist. Therefore, major literary research has focused on the male characters whereas the woman-figure has largely escaped notice. In my opinion the female characters in these novels, even if they occupy rather minor roles, relate back to and take their strength from their mythic prototypes in southwestern creation stories. It is on the surface only that the novels of Momaday and Silko appear to be the stories of alienated Native American men; at closer proximity they turn out to be accounts of female power as preserved in mythology and acknowledged through symbolism and ceremony.

Despite the devastation and suppression suffered in wars and conquest, not conflict and disruption but transformation and continuance are the novels' central themes. Allen, Momaday, and Silko achieve this continuity through their ability to reach back, regardless of time and space, to the powerful female creator-goddesses of mythology. It is the oftentimes hard-won capacity to not only reconnect with but **relive** the past that eventually transforms and heals the protagonists and, as in Silko's Ceremony, all of society.

While the mythic dimension of the male protagonists will not be overlooked and, as in Momaday's novels, will be reevaluated, emphasis will be placed on the mythic properties of the female characters. Since "the tendency to equal distribution of value among all elements," as Allen asserts, "is an integral part of tribal consciousness," since there are "no minor characters, and foreground slips along from one focal point to another until all the pertinent elements in the ritual conversation have had their say,"[14] this dissertation will now listen to some mythic voices long ignored.

II. Historical Survey or "The West Wasn't Wild Until the Whites Came"[1]

i.

the United States

> Some researchers put the pre-contact population at more than 45 million, while others put it at around 20 million. The U.S. government long put it at 450,000 - a comforting if imaginary figure, though at one point it was put at around 270,000. If the current population is around one million [and] if the average life expectancy is, as the best-informed research presently says, 55 years;[2] if the infant mortality rate continues at well above national standards; if the average unemployment for all segments of population - male, female, young, adult, and middle-aged, is between 60 and 90 percent; if the U.S. government continues its policy of termination, relocation, removal, and assimilation along with the destruction of wilderness, reservation land, and its resources, and severe curtailment of hunting, fishing, timber harvesting and water-use rights - then existing tribes are facing the threat of extinction which for several hundred tribal groups has already become fact in the past five hundred years.[3]

Neither scope nor purpose of this book allow a complete discussion of the calamities that have threatened and continue to threaten Native Americans. However, the impact of certain events--especially those concerning the collapse of women's power in tribal societies--should neither be overlooked nor underestimated. In order to understand both the resignation of Native Americans and the renewal of ancestral structures and beliefs (both are central aspects of the novels to be discussed), it is necessary to examine what happens to cultures and their mythologies on the brink of disintegration.

Paula Gunn Allen insists that most western studies of Native American tribal systems "are erroneous at base because they inevitably view tribalism from the cultural bias of patriarchy and thus either discount, degrade, or conceal gynocratic features or recontextualize those features so that they will appear patriarchal." She further maintains that the colonial powers have exerted their influence "to remove Indian women from every position of authority, to obliterate all records pertaining to gynocratic social systems, and to ensure that no American and few American Indians would remember that gynocracy was the primary social order of Indian America prior to 1800."[4]

> However he is viewed - sympathetically or with suspicion and terror - the Indian is always *he*. Certainly *she* never rides tall and noble in the saddle, face framed in savage splendor with plundered feathers of great fighting birds. *She* never parlays in powwow council with the white man, offering the peace pipe/calumet to the gods, asking that the proceedings be blessed by heathen powers. *She* never dies at Sand Creek or Wounded Knee. *She* is not the old shaman who gives advice to the young and sends them to the mountains to find their vision; *she* does not have the visions that tell of a nation's destruction. *She* does not stand on the top of a bluff weeping for the broken hoop of the nation. *She* is not revered in the memory of Americans as shaman, warrior-chief, peacemaker.[5]

The story of the Iroquois (Haudenashonee), which is also the story of the breakdown of women's status in tribal communities as a result of colonization, constitutes a prime example of a complete restructuring of tribal identity. Iroquois is the name given to the North American Indian confederacy that was formed around the middle of the fifteenth century. The League was founded by the legendary Deganawidah who set out on a journey "to stop the shedding of blood among human beings." The Constitution of the Five Nations clearly reflects the central role women played: "The lineal descent of the people of the Five Nations shall run in the female line. Women shall be considered the progenitors of the Nation. They shall own the land and the soil. Men and women shall follow the status of the mother."[6]

Property and goods were inherited entirely through the female line. The women owned both the living quarters as well as the garden plots (even though they were cleared by men). The children always belonged to the mother's lineage. Although in the political sphere they did not implement policies, women had the sole power to appoint and to remove from office. In warfare they had the power of life or death over prisoners. They also helped to select the religious practitioners known as "keepers of the faith," and half of these had to be females. Peter Farb explains the power enjoyed by females with their ritual and economic centrality:

> They were sedentary horticulturists while the males were nomadic - nearly always away making war, hunting, trapping, or trading. Iroquois women not only totally controlled the lands they cultivated, the implements they used, and the seed supply. They also maintained the right to distribute all food, even that obtained by males through hunting. The females could thus prevent the formation of a war party, if they disagreed with the action, by withholding supplies of dried corn needed for the expedition. In other words, the unusually high status of females is not explainable as some historical curiosity but rather as the direct result of controlling the economic foundations of the tribe.[7]

Yet, to the extent that the power of the colonizers and missionaries increased during the late Colonial period, the women's ceremonial and economic influence lessened.

The Cherokee suffered a similar fate. Carolyn Foreman reiterates John Adair's remarks on the Cherokee: "The Cherokee had been for a considerable while under petticoat government and they were just emerging, like all of the

Iroquoian Indians from the matriarchal period." Adair's idea of a "petticoat government" referred to the power of the Women's Council of the Cherokee, the head of which was the Beloved Woman of the Nation, "whose voice was considered that of the Great Spirit, speaking through her."[8]

The British government was in many ways responsible for the oftentimes complete restructuring of tribal organizations which inevitably resulted in the weakened power of women in Cherokee affairs. Since only Cherokee men were taken to England to be educated in the ways of European democracy, naturally only men could exert great influence on behalf of the British upon their return. By the time Congress debated the **Indian Removal Act** in the early nineteenth century, many of these British-educated men held considerable power over Cherokee policies as leaders, interpreters, or partners in negotiations.[9] Not only most eastern tribes but also the Plains cultures were--contrary to their reputation--matrifocal. "Because of the stereotypes that have been created," says the Kiowa author and Pulitzer Prize winner N. Scott Momaday, "people really do think of the plains cultures as patriarchal. That's a false view. It is true that men were most visible in those societies. But that is not to say that the women were less important."[10]

The documented sources concerning women's economic and religious power in history are inexplicable without a thorough knowledge of the tribes' origin stories. Before these mythic tales will ever gain relevance as important historical documentation, however, there needs to be a complete reevaluation concerning the historical value of myths: they need to be regarded not as tales concerning a long forgotten past, but as an entrance to realities otherwise not accessible anymore. The insignificance most historians attach to myths might serve as one reason why little is known concerning the matrifocal structure of native societies. The failure of important historians to include documented information concerning the high-status position of women in the leadership structure of native tribes "reinforces patriarchal socialization among all Americans, who are thus led to believe that there have never been any alternative structures." In addition, it gives Anglo-Europeans the idea that Native American societies were "beneath the level of organization of western nations, justifying colonization by presumption of lower stature. . . ."[11] Allen lists the steps used to alter the foundations of tribal existence: first, "the foundations of tribal governing institutions and the philosophies of that area are destroyed" and the conquerors demand "that the tribes that wish federal recognition and protection institute 'democracy,' in which powerful officials are elected by majority vote." Then,

> the people are pushed off their lands, deprived of their economic livelihood, and forced to curtail or end altogether pursuits on which their ritual system, philosophy, and subsistence depend. Now dependant on white institutions for survival, tribal systems can ill afford gynocracy when patriarchy - that is, survival - requires male dominance.[12]

The **Indian Removal Act** of 1830 under the direction of the **Bureau of Indian Affairs** (**BIA**)--established in 1824 as part of the **War Department**--was the first official attempt to separate Native Americans from their ancestral lands. Andrew Jackson's promise to the eastern tribes that beyond the Mississippi "their father has provided a country large enough for them all," and that there "their white brothers will not trouble them [and] they can live upon it . . . as long as grass grows and waters run"[13] had far reaching consequences. Since mythologies develop around and are connected to specific geographies, the forced removal was more than a mere territorial displacement. By ordering the eviction of almost all Native Americans east of the Mississippi into the lands of the West, the **Removal Act** initiated the long process of social and spiritual disintegration among the eastern tribes.

The forced midwinter marches also led to the infamous **Trail of Tears** where four thousand Cherokees died due to food rationing, coldness, and a vastly different territory which bore diseases hitherto unknown to them. The great removal was not the panacea its advocates in Congress had promised it would be. Since the tribes west of the Mississippi had to give up some of their lands to make room for the newcomers, they were hostile toward the eastern tribes. Clashes between various tribal groups became increasingly common. In addition, the United States government soon discovered the natural resources of the West. As Farb states, "miners and settlers were on the move, emigrant trains rumbled across the plains, and once again the aim of the frontiersman, bringing with him the railroad, guns, plows, fences, plagues, alcohol, and the Bible, was to get the Indians out of the way."[14]

Although the romanticist movement of the nineteenth century opposed the violent extermination of primal cultures, its simplistic glorification of the past did not further the Native American cause. The ignoble "savage" became noble, and primal people were now depicted as naturally good and unspoiled by the ravages of civilization. Thus, they had to adapt themselves to either one of two impossible images--innocence or evil--leaving them no space to live as they had lived before.

The last fifty years of the nineteenth century marked a time of great uphkeaval in Native American life. The Sun Dance, for instance--one of the most important rituals of the Plains tribes--and the Ghost Dance--the movement that had led to the massacre at Wounded Knee--had been outlawed and the southern and northern herds of buffalo had been completely destroyed.[15] Describing his grandmother's life in <u>House Made of Dawn</u>, Tosamah, "orator, physician, Priest of the Sun, son of Hummingbird" (HMD 117), gives a graphic account of those disastrous events:

> She was a Christian in her later years . . . but she never forgot her birthright. As a child, she had been to the sun dances; she had taken part in that annual rite, and by it she had learned the restoration of her people in the presence of Tai-me [the sun dance doll, the most sacred fetish of the Kiowa]. She was about seven years old when the

> last Kiowa sun dance was held in 1887 on the Washita River above Rainy Mountain Creek. The buffalo were gone. In order to consummate the ancient sacrifice -to impale the head of a buffalo bull upon the Tai-me tree - a delegation of old men journeyed into Texas, there to beg and barter for an animal. . . . She was ten when the Kiowas came together for the last time as a living sun dance culture. They could find no buffalo; they had to hang an old hide from the sacred tree. . . . Forbidden without cause the essential act of their faith, having seen the wild herds slaughtered and left to rot upon the ground, the Kiowas backed away forever from the tree. That was July 20, 1890, at the great bend of the Washita. My grandmother was there. Without bitterness, and for as long as she lived, she bore a vision of deicide (HMD 121-122).

With the establishment of reservations in 1851 (a government measure that replaced the policy of removal), the importance of women began to change even more dramatically. Once reservation life as well as the diminished number of buffalo restricted the men's freedom of mobility--thus depriving them of their ancestral roles as hunters and warriors--they began to move into areas previously dominated by women. Towards the end of the nineteenth century, off-reservation schools for native youngsters were established.[16] All over the country the boarding schools, which were allowed to take in children without the consent of their relatives, were often located at great distances from the reservations--probably in an attempt to force young Native Americans to break with their heritage. Now the children's upbringing was in the hands of public schools rather than the responsibility of parents and grandparents. As Silko relates in Ceremony, any ritual bonding to tribal beliefs was undermined when home-economics teachers told girls to dress "exactly like the white girls" (C 69), while the science teacher "explained exactly what superstition was, and then held the science textbook up for the clans to see the true source of explanation" (C 94). With the men at home and the children gone, women were stripped of their economic centrality and their influence as parental guides. However, since major tribal ceremonies had been outlawed--thereby curtailing or even eradicating any ritual expression--it is not unlikely that the origin stories and related legends, often told by women in the confines of their homes, now received even greater attention. Thus, while the ceremonial power of men certainly decreased, women were in a position to continue the upholding of traditional tales. Thereby, they not only maintained, but possibly even empowered, their roles as the tribes' spiritual repository.

The **Dawes Severalty Act** of 1887, which assigned small plots of land to individuals, reflected the assimilationist tendency of the U.S. government. In addition to again losing vast areas of their territories, Native American lifeways had to undergo new changes when individual farming was required of communal hunters. The incidents on the Sioux Reservation provide an example of land loss and tribal displacement not uncommon among Native American tribes. The U.S. government and the Sioux chief Red Cloud had signed a treaty in 1868, affirming the Sioux property of 18 million acres of reservation land. Shortly afterwards, however, General Custer discovered "the yellow metal that makes the wasichu [white man] crazy"[17] in the Black Hills. Black Elk, the Oglala Sioux medicine man, remembers the year 1876:

> Wherever we went the soldiers came to kill us, and it was all our own country. It was ours already when the Wasichus made the treaty with Red Cloud that said it would be ours as long as grass should grow and water flow. That was only eight winters before, and they were chasing us now because we remembered and they forgot.[18]

When the **Sioux Act** of 1889 halved the Lakota lands once again, transferring nine million acres to the newly-arrived settlers, it directly violated the aforementioned treaty, and left the Sioux no choice but to further abandon their original way of life.

In the last three decades of the nineteenth century, the fighting between Native Americans and whites increased. One after the other, the tribes rose in rebellion only to be defeated--the southern Plains tribes in 1874, the Sioux in 1876, the Nez Perce in 1877, the Cheyenne and Bannock in 1878, the Ute in 1879, and the Apache until Geronimo surrendered with his remnant band of thirty-six survivors towards the end of the century. These were, as Farb believes, "the final spasms of a people who had long before been defeated logistically and psychologically."[19] In the context of the barbarous ferocity on both sides, Allen calls for a reevaluation of the cultural traditions of Native America,

> because as long as they are seen as braves and warriors the fiction that they were conquered in a fair and just war will be upheld. It is in the interest of the United States - along with the other political entities in the western hemisphere to maintain that foolish and tragic deception; and thus the focus has long been on Indians as noble or savage warriors who, as it happens, lost the war to superior military competence.[20]

The establishment of reservations and boarding schools enabled Anglo missionaries and United States Indian Bureau officials to concentrate on the eradication of "un-American" customs and practices. Furthermore, the **Bureau of Indian Affairs** also made a number of attempts to suppress native tradition with a series of departmental regulations. What had started as a reaction to both the Sun Dance and the Ghost Dance movement culminated in a set of regulations known as the **Code of Religious Offenses** in 1889. The number of participants was restricted, age limits were set, and ceremonial practices considered offensive to accepted Christian standards were forbidden.

It was not until 1934 that the policy of religious repression was reversed. Under John Collier's administration the following directive was issued: "No interference with Indian religious life or ceremonial expression will hereafter be tolerated. The cultural liberty of Indians is in all respects to be considered equal to that of any non-Indian group."[21] The freedom of religion, at least on paper, was finally extended to North America's original inhabitants. Yet, even in the last decades of the twentieth century, religious freedom stands as an ideal hardly achieved. N. Scott Momaday said in an interview:

> Of course the Catholic church could not approve of the Indian religion, but it certainly was aware of the Indian religion. It could not accept or condone it. Consequently, there was always a religious tension in the pueblos. When I was living at Jemez I was aware of that tension, and of course reflected it in House Made of Dawn.[22]

Forced to abandon their native visionaries and discard their belief in the ancestral spirit world, Native Americans gave in to Christianity--many not out of conviction but necessity. Whole clans tended to join the same church regardless of denomination. Often such membership simply meant the obtainment of ration books and access to clothing and shelter. Baum, the German translator of Momaday's The Way to Rainy Mountain, notes that '. .. religious convictions were and (still) are considered a very personal experience to the Native American. Oftentimes, Native Americans had themselves baptized out of politeness in order not to insult the pushy missionaries'.[23] The lay catechists often moved from one denomination to the next because of better pay or a new place to live. Quite frequently the medicine men became important Christian functionaries. Well-known ones, like Black Elk, served for brief periods as lay readers in both Catholic and Episcopal churches. For him--as for many others--being a Christian had nothing to do with spiritual convictions; instead, as Powers affirms, it was an economic, political, and social means to an end.[24]

In 1979 the **American Indian Religious Freedom Act** was passed, permitting Native Americans to practice their traditional rituals and ceremonies once again. Yet, over a hundred years after the establishment of reservations many

Native Americans "are still caught between cultures, living the worst conditions of both."

> Their lands contain half the uranium and one-third the strip mine coal in the United States (the coal alone worth perhaps a trillion dollars), and yet with unemployment, suicide, and alcoholism rates soaring some reservations suffer the worst hardship in North America . . . .

An even more serious oppression, Lincoln believes, threatens Native Americans today under "melting-pot policies of assimilation, and the direct and indirect coercion of tribes to adapt to mainstream U.S. culture."[25] The result is that "many people are trapped between tribal values constituting their unconscious behavior responses and the values that they have been taught in schools and churches, which primarily demand conforming to seemingly foreign ideals." Among minorities, Native Americans are "the only group," as Deloria further notes, "whose oppression comes primarily from an effort to help them change into replicas of the white man."[26]

In order to emphasize the necessity of transforming the Native Americans into whites, the printed media and Hollywood's movies have continually fostered the stereotype of the "red savage." In his recollections The Names, N. Scott Momaday remembers the effects of the media on his own imagination:

> I will shoot an Indian down by the creek he will see me but I will see him first and I will wait until he sees me it has to be that way of course . . . and his mouth is open and he is **ugly** of course he has a knife it is a great big knife . . . he has of course killed many men women and children with the knife and . . . he smiles and he is even uglier so it is you at last he says and I nod . . . I shoot him and nimbly I catch the knife in the stock of my gun over my heart and the ugly Indian staggers and slumps and pitches headfirst into a ravine and I say you're dead and of course it is so[27]

In its exploration and exploitation of the image of the "vanishing savage," the news and entertainment industries have almost entirely focused on the male. Due to the nearly complete disruption of their lifeways which consisted mainly of trade, hunting, and tribal warfare, Native American men are more suited than native women to fulfill the notion of the desolate hero. While Native American women have suffered tremendous losses in the political sphere, their responsibility towards their homes and immediate surroundings--although greatly lessened--to this day nevertheless provides a certain continuity regardless of historical events. This, in turn, has enabled them to keep an influential position within the family and social structure. The nature of "women's role" has thus permitted the cultural lives of Native American women to be more fully sustained than the lives of men. "Consequently," writes Antell, "Indian men more than Indian women can be seen as tragic figures who have clearly suffered the more severe losses, albeit inevitable and ultimately desirable losses in the assessment of the dominant society." While Native American men present the more "tragic" figures in a dramatic sense, they also, through the same process, provide the greater comfort to the dominant society; a comfort which results from the firm belief that Native Americans really have changed.[28]

While the lives of Native American men represent change and a clear separation from the past, the lives of Native American women manifest the continuance of at least part of their cultural identity. More important than women's centrality within the familial sphere, this heritage includes women's lasting linkage and sustained identification with the events and characters of mythic times. As repositories of traditional stories and ideals, women uphold the religious stability of their respective tribes through their spiritual and generative powers. Allen, Momaday, and Silko explore both the bonding with and the continuance of the mythic past as a major source of women's strength and endurance. Since it is this tie to the myths of tribal heritage that ensures Native American spiritual and physical survival, their novels are "a major part of Indian resistance to cultural and spiritual genocide."[29]

ii.

the Southwest

The roots of the sedentary Pueblo cultures in the Southwest reach back to the big game (Mammoth) hunters of around 12,000 B.C. and to a variety of desert cultures, the most recent of which--the Hohokam and the Anasazis--intermingled around 1400 A.D. Whereas the Hohokam are known for their art, their stone etchings, jewelry, and figurine pottery, the culture of the Basket Makers, or Anasazi (a Navajo word meaning "the ancient ones") attained their cultural peak with the construction of the multi-storied "apartment buildings" at Mesa Verde and Chaco Canyon around 1100 A.D.[1] Since these times, the peoples of the Southwest have developed complex cultures identified with their specific habitat.

The Pueblos can be grouped into three distinct and different language families with diverse origins. These language families are Keresan, Tanoan, and Zunian. The Tanoan language is further divided into three dialects: Tewa, Tiwa, and Towa.[2] The ceremonial structure contrasts rather dramatically from the Hopi lands in the west to the Rio Grande Pueblos in the east. Ceremonies for rain are emphasized at Hopi; curing and rain-making rituals receive equal attention at Zuni; and at Acoma and Laguna the concern for attaining health and well-being clearly prevails.

Whereas the western and the Keresan Pueblos emphasize matrilineal exogamous clans, female ownership of house and garden plots, and a matrilocal residence, matrilineal clans within the eastern (or Rio Grande) Pueblo structure are weak. Traditional kinship behavior among the western Pueblos functions as follows: the women are the important members of the unit; they own the house and are responsible for the preparation and distribution of food. They also care for the ritual possessions of the family. Men born into the household and lineage leave the house when they marry, although they return frequently and exercise considerable authority in religious matters. In traditional families the husbands contribute to the economic support of the household, but leave disciplinary and economic decisions to their wives and their wives' brothers and uncles. It should be noted, however, that many families in both eastern as well as western Pueblos have chosen to abandon the traditional kinship behavior, preferring instead the U.S. model in which the husband functions as head of the family. As will be shown below, the western Pueblos had far less contact with Christian missionaries and government agencies. Therefore, their societal structure remained more intact than that of the eastern Pueblos. This might serve as an explanation for the lower-profile role of women within the eastern Pueblo organization.[3]

The Athabascan (Na-Dinė)-speaking Navajos appeared in the Southwest as recently as A.D. 1200-1541, having migrated south from their homeland in the Yukon-Mackenzie subarctic area.[4] Owing to their hunting and gathering economy, the Navajos were able to exist in small groups. It is likely that the earliest of them coming into New Mexico populated the villages and adjoining lands earlier abandoned by the Pueblos. Through sporadic contact with the Pueblos, the Navajos slowly modified their hunting-gathering organization and acquired horticultural knowledge which eventually led to a semisedentary resident pattern. Both linguistically and ceremonially the Kiowa, although a Plains tribe, share many similarities with southwestern cultures. Since "the Kiowa of the eighteenth and nineteenth centuries used to make raids into the Pueblo territory" and "had trade relation with the Pueblos,"[5] ritual fragments have undoubtedly circulated and parallels in ceremonialism, even if slight, are thus obvious between the Kiowa Plains tribe and the Navajo and Pueblo tribes of the Southwest.

There still exists considerable disagreement as to the origin of the Navajos' matrifocality. Whereas some scholars believe that the indigenous Navajo system was woman-centered, others insist that "in the space of a few years the Navaho adopted the Puebloan styles of architecture, manufacturing techniques, and religious paraphernalia, plus many elements of non-material culture such as clans, matrilineal descent, matrilocal residence, the origin myth, and ritual."[6] In any event, the Navajo social system, like that of their Pueblo neighbors, is organized in clans with descent and inheritance traced through the maternal line. Not only matrilineal descent, but also matrilocality are emphasized in traditional Navajo households. The anthropologist Gladys Reichard writes that women's "status in the home, in the economic, social, even political life is equal to that of men." Since they or their mothers own the house and property, separation from unwanted partners is easy for Navajo women. When Set in Momaday's The Ancient Child, asks about Grey's Navajo brother-in-law, she answers: "My sister threw him away" (AC 269). Reichard further explains that socially,

> the position of the Navajo woman is high. She has a voice in all family affairs and many times her decision on a matter is final since she may have control of the family pursestrings according to the relative wealth of herself and her husband. It should not be inferred however that wealth is the main cause of the woman's high prestige. For she is held in general regard and the feeling of the family for her opinion is something which one finds difficult to describe.[7]

The search for Cibola, rumored to have been a province home to seven cities of silver and gold, brought the Spanish conquistadors to the Southwest. A series of explorations, begun in 1539 by Fray Marcos de Niza, "failed to locate anything more spectacular than villages of mud and stone inhabited by people rich in ceremonialism but poor in material possessions."[8] Not fundamentally opposed to warfare, counterattacks by the Pueblo tribes were nevertheless considered disturbing to the normal order of life. A return to daily routine was of utmost importance, not necessarily the destruction of the enemy. In this context, Tyler refers to a war chief who "asked the American cavalry to retire and not disturb the normal social processes of Hopi life," and a Zuni war chief who "used a whistle - a clarion call to the supernaturals - which was supposed to disperse the Spanish military."[9]

Formal colonization of New Mexico was begun in 1598 under the leadership of Don Juan de Onate. The Pueblo tribes were required to swear obedience to the King of Spain and the Catholic church. Missionaries were forced on most of the tribes. The Spaniards also imposed the **Law of the Indies** which decreed that each village elect a governor and other officials to handle secular affairs. Tribute was demanded in the form of food or textiles. As compensation each Pueblo received a Spanish name and military protection. Of far greater importance to the tribes, however, was the acquisition of new tools, different kinds of fruit trees, and new domestic plants and animals. Since the Navajos were still organized in semi-nomadic groups at that time, they initially escaped formal subordination through the Spanish.

The Pueblo tribes appear to have absorbed very few Catholic beliefs and values during the first century of contact with Spanish culture and the Catholic religion. They performed the external acts required of them, such as Mass attendance and Holy Communion. Some were baptized, married, and buried by the missionaries. Such acts, Dozier notes, were done under compulsion and it is unlikely that any of the church concepts were really understood and internalized. Instead, the efforts to eradicate the old folk customs merely drove the Pueblos deeper into their own indigenous religion:

> The Pueblos were not unwilling to accept externals of the new faith, but they found it difficult to understand the deeper spiritual values of Christianity. Pueblo religion served definite material and social ends, viz., the propitiation of those supernatural forces which they believed controlled their daily existence. They expected the same results from the Christian faith. But they soon realized that the new ways were no more successful in obtaining a good harvest than the old, and they realized too that the efforts to abolish their traditional ceremonials

> and destroy the influence of the old native leaders whose functions were both social and religious, raised serious problems concerning the entire fund of Pueblo civilization. Bewilderment soon turned into resentment and resentment into resurgence of loyalty to the traditional norms of folk-culture.[10]

The disintegration of their societies under military and cultural domination made the Pueblo tribes yearn for the way of life they had once known. The rise of the Taoan prophet Popé, who promised a return to the past and doom for the white intruders, was the inevitable result of the increasing hostility, eventually leading to the **Pueblo Revolt** of 1680. It became clear that only a united effort of the Pueblos could overthrow the conquistadors. Such unity was difficult to achieve within the individually organized Pueblo communities. Furthermore, resistance to warfare against the invaders was widespread due to the tribes' knowledge of their legends. Many southwestern prophecies tell of the tribes' creation of "bahana," the white man or woman. *Naotsete*, later called *Sun Woman*, for example, went east to create the white race. I remember *Sun Woman*, Allen writes, "who held metals and cattle, pigs and sheep, highways and engines and so many things in her bundle, who went away to the east saying that one day she would return."[11] Having brought with them many plants, animals, and items necessary for all aspects of domestic life, the Spanish invaders were often considered descendants of the original Keres goddess, thereby making the myths come true. However, after dominion became increasingly more unbearable, the tribes for once cooperated and managed to drive out the Spaniards who retreated to El Paso. Until 1692 the Pueblos once again functioned as autonomous entities. After almost a century of forced labor and church attendances, of constantly "sweeping and putting the missions in order," the Pueblos, Hacketts writes, had finally driven out their oppressors.[12]

Although the united effort was a success, unity collapsed when Popé attempted to become the unchallenged leader of all the Pueblo tribes. The

Pueblos' larger tribal organization was simply too fragile and new to survive for long in a more complex political system. The confederation soon broke apart and tribes began warring among themselves. Under Diego de Vargas the Spaniards marched back and reconquered the Pueblos in 1692, re-establishing Spanish authority in New Mexico.

Throughout the years before, during, and after the **Pueblo Revolt**, the Navajos and Pueblos had had significant contact. In some instances it is likely that the Pueblos, resentful of growing Spanish pressures, encouraged Navajo raids.[13] Also, due to Spanish attacks after the reconquest of 1692, many of the Pueblos were abandoned, and the inhabitants were driven northward toward the San Juan, which brought them into close proximity with the Navajos.

Under Spanish rule the number of Pueblos in the Rio Grande valley decreased from sixty-six in 1540 to nineteen in 1700. In the same span of time the native population was reduced by half.[14] New diseases, particularly periodic smallpox epidemics, were the main cause of population diminution. Speaking of the origin of the Eagle Watchers Society in House Made of Dawn, Momaday writes that they "were a wretched people" from the Tanoan city of Bahkyula. Their land bordered upon the southern Plains where,

> for many years they had been an easy mark for marauding bands of buffalo hunters and thieves. They had endured every kind of persecution until one day they could stand no more and their spirit broke. They gave themselves up to despair and were then at the mercy of the first alien wind. But it was not a human enemy that overcame them at last; it was a plague. They were struck down by so deadly a disease that when the epidemic abated, there were fewer than twenty survivors in all (HMD 18).

Spain's power in the New World weakened progressively towards the end of the eighteenth century. She was unable to continue the domination of the

Pueblos (especially the western communities) that she had maintained during the seventeenth and the first half of the eighteenth century. With the suppression of their religious rites relaxed, the Pueblos were again enjoying a rich ceremonial life. Although disturbing to the friars, they did not possess the authority to stop them. The isolation of the western Pueblos from the center of the provincial government became even more pronounced when Mexico gained its independence from Spain in 1821. This resulted in the transference of jurisdiction over New Mexico from Spain to Mexico. The new rulers, unlike Spain, bestowed full rights of citizenship upon the southwestern tribes. Contact with the western Pueblos virtually ceased until late in the nineteenth century when the United States government established relations with them.

The **Treaty of Guadalupe Hidalgo** (1848) marked the end of the Mexican-American war and transferred New Mexican territory to the United States. It bound the U.S. to respect the land rights of all former citizens of Mexico. When the United States assumed jurisdiction over the southwestern tribes, the land grants of all but the western Pueblos of Zuni and Hopi had been invaded by the constant flow of settlers and disputes which were not resolved until the mid-1930s began. In 1849 jurisdiction over Native Americans was shifted from the **War Department** to the **Bureau of Indian Affairs** (under the **Department of the Interior**) where it remains until today.

Belonging now to the jurisdiction of the United States, the isolated life of the southwestern tribes began to change with accelerated speed as more settlers and missionaries moved west. Towards the end of the nineteenth century, United States proceeded with their intensive campaigns against the Comanche, the Navajos, and the various bands of Apaches. Dutton writes that, "all captives who surrendered voluntarily would be taken [to Fort Sumner] and all male Navaho who resisted were to be shot. Their livestock and food supplies were to be destroyed; and they were."[15] Like all over North America, Native American resistance to the better armed government soldiers came to an end during the last years of the nineteenth century. All of the nomadic tribes had been placed on reservations and the "Indian menace" was over. The following instructions to Colonel Kit Carson who had been placed in charge of removing the Navajos, expresses the policy of extermination generally shared by military commanders:

> The Indian men . . . are to be killed whenever and wherever you can find them: the women and children will not be harmed, but you will take them prisoners. . . . If the Indians send in a flag and desire to treat for peace, say to the bearer; [they have broken] their treaty of peace, and murdered innocent people and run off their stock: that now we are going to punish them for their crimes, and that you are there to kill them wherever they can be found. We have no faith in their broken promises and we intend to kill enough of their men to teach them a lesson.[16]

The effect of both the policies of the United States and the behavior of Anglo missionaries on southwestern culture was profound. The Rio Grande Pueblos reintrenched their native ceremonial system much as they had during the seventeenth century when Spanish oppression and attacks on native religion were particularly severe. In the Pueblos of Zuni and Hopi, the severity of religious persecution had been forgotten and their initial response to contact with Euro-Americans was friendly. As government agents and missionaries began to proselytize and to prohibit some of their sacred rites, however, they too went back into secrecy, strictly guarding the most sacred aspects of their religious system. In <u>House Made of Dawn</u>, Father Olguin remarks in a diary entry from the year 1874 that

> Tomacita Fragua died this late morning & again I was not called to it. But the son-in-law Diego came in the afternoon & gave me leave to make the burial. I saw they had finished with her according to

> their dark custom & there was blue and yellow meal about on the floor (HMD 47).

The impact of Christianity upon native southwestern religion is difficult to summarize except in generalizations. A minority accepted the new religion to the complete abandonment of native practices. A majority merely accommodated the new doctrines by modifying them to fit with native beliefs; this was primarily the case with the Rio Grande Pueblos. "The Pueblos are quite happy being Catholics and Kachina worshipers at one and the same time," according to Lame Deer. "I know of one Catholic saint whom they made into a Kachina rain god, and they tell me he's doing fine at that job."[17] Many Pueblo Indians modified Catholicism into a form that suited their own needs but was not recognized by the churches. In House Made of Dawn, Father Olguin complains to his brother about Francisco, one of the villagers:

> He is one of them & goes often in the kiva & and puts on their horns & and hides & does worship that Serpent which even is the One our most ancient enemy. He is unashamed to make one of my sacristans & brother I am most fearful to forbid it. You will be reviled I believe to hear that he lays hold of the paten & the Host & so defiles me in the sight of my enemies. Where is the Most Holy Spirit that he is not struck down at that moment? I have some expectation of it always & am disappointed (HMD 50-51).

Others, such as the followers of the Native American Church, a.k.a. the Peyote Cult, combine native and Christian beliefs to form an entirely new religious movement. Of course, a surprising number, notably among the Hopi and the Zuni, practice their native religion to the total exclusion of Christian beliefs:

> The people of the town have little need. They do not hanker after progress and have never changed their essential way of life. Their invaders were a long time in conquering them; and now, after four

> centuries of Christianity, they still pray . . . to the old deities of the earth and sky and make their living from the things that are and have always been within their reach; while in the discrimination of pride they acquire from their conquerors only the luxury of example. They have assumed the names and gestures of their enemies, but have held on to their own, secret souls; and in this there is a resistance and an overcoming, a long outwaiting (HMD 56).

The Pueblos and the Navajos exercised different ways of dealing with those outside threats from the Spanish explorers and military, the Christian missionaries, and the North American government agencies. The Pueblos learned the wisdom of appearing to succumb to Christian views while abiding in secret by their own traditional beliefs and sacred rites. As with Pueblo traditions before, the Navajos, on the other hand, considered the incorporation of some ceremonial changes introduced by the newcomers not in disharmony with their own ritualistic framework.

Compared to other North American tribes, the Pueblo and Navajo tribal organizations have remained relatively untouched by the detraditionalizing influences exerted by various political and religious groups. More than in other native communities, their tribal structures survive until today. Due to their ability to either continue their rites and ceremonies in secret or incorporate spiritual changes into the body of their ceremonial practices, southwestern tribes have not experienced the severe cultural loss endured by many eastern and northeastern tribes. The social, religious, and economic transformations have not been abrupt, and many Navajo and Pueblo groups, "shielded from the ever-intensifying and multi-form missionary attack in the isolated parts of their large reservation" still see the world "as bounded by four sacred mountains and their place in it as influenced by spirits who had come up from an underworld."[18]

III. Philosophical/Mythological Survey

i.
philosophy

Native American literature is based on philosophical principles which are intimately tied to native beliefs about the structure of the universe. Due to the particular quality of native beliefs there exists the necessity for reevaluating present Native American philosophical-literary traditions and, in the process, "to free them from outmoded prejudices that are revealed in such loaded polar terms as primitive and progressive, backward and developed, literate and illiterate."[1]

Like most native people adhering to traditional beliefs, the Native American of the American Southwest perceives life as balanced and interdependent. Ceremonies are performed to "convince" nature to respond with the essentials of life, hopefully withholding disasters. This ideal equilibrium is fragile and may change at any time through a) the violation of taboos, b) harboring evil thoughts, c) initiating or being the victim of acts of witchcraft, or, d) disrespect in one's relationship with the forces of the natural world. "The consequences of imbalance," according to Dozier, "are most often illness, disasters, and drought. Rites and ceremonies properly performed," on the other hand, "keep the seasons moving, allow the sun to rise and set properly, bring rain and snow, quell the winds and insure a well-ordered physical environment and society."[2]

The concept most pervasive and basic to Native American traditions is the belief in the ultimate wholeness of existence. In their refusal to divide the material and the spiritual--both of which are perceived as twin manifestations of the same reality--Native American traditions stress the interrelatedness of even diverse categories. Since all things are complementary the distinction between animate and inanimate, or between animal, plant, and mineral has no meaning in a tribal context; instead, **all** that exists is animated. Calling this phenomenon "magical thinking," the German philosopher Jürgen Habermas says:

> Magisches Denken erlaubt keine grundbegriffliche Unterscheidung zwischen Dingen und Personen, Unbeseeltem und Beseeltem, zwischen Gegenständen, die manipuliert werden können, und Agenten, denen wir Handlungen und sprachliche Äußerungen zurechnen.[3]

Another concept related to the complementary order of native traditions is found in the experience of time and process. They are generally understood not in the linear manner but in terms of the "sacred hoop," that is, cyclical and reciprocal. The span of both human and nonhuman life, just like the seasons of nature, are understood to form a cycle and are expressed through a variety of ceremonial acts.[4] Black Elk perceives the wholeness of existence in the cyclical nature of his environment:

> Everything the Power of the World does is done in a circle. The sky is round, and I have heard that the earth is round like a ball, and so are all the stars. The wind, in its greatest power, whirls. Birds make their nests in circles, for theirs is the same religion as ours. The sun comes forth and goes down again in a circle. The moon does the same, and both are round. Even the seasons form a great circle in their changing, and always come back again to where they were. The life of a man is a circle from childhood to childhood, and so it is in everything where power moves. Our tepees were round like the nests of birds, and these were always set in a circle, the nation's hoop, a nest of many nests, where the Great Spirit meant for us to hatch our children.[5]

The clock, the very embodiment of the western concept of time, functions in contemporary southwestern literature as the mechanized, unnatural counterpart to the sun, the traditional time-keeping force among primal peoples of the American Southwest. The concept of time, not as a linear succession of events, but as a nonlinear continuum of experience in an infinite frame of time and space, marks a unique quality of native perspectives on literature.

The highly individuated concept of self testifies to a noteworthy difference between western and Native American concepts of existence. Primal cultures are based on tribal rather than individual experience. North American tribes "possess what must be called a 'communal soul' in comparison with the Western precept of the soul as personal property that ensures, under certain moral regulations, the eternal perpetuation of the private ego."[6] Even among the Navajo tribe, the community most concerned with individual well-being among primal cultures, any preoccupation with the individual results from the belief that a person out of balance will negatively affect the whole tribal group. "The possibility of conceiving of an individual alone in a tribal religious sense is ridiculous," writes Deloria. "The very complexity of tribal life and the interdependence of people on one another makes this conception improbable at best, a terrifying loss of identity at worst."[7] In tribal religions there is no salvation apart from the continuance of the tribe itself because the existence of the individual presupposes the existence of the community.

Creation in native traditions is the joint effort of a creator-figure assisted by co-creators. Creation is a matter of "shared power" which helps to explain why--as opposed to monotheistic tradition--there might be a prevailing, but hardly an absolute, deity. Both the Navajo goddess *Changing Woman* and her Pueblo counterpart *Thought Woman* voluntarily shared their divine abilities after the initial act of creation. Most creation myths describe animals and plants not only as helpmates and saviors of humans, but as co-creators of the world. The Iroquois goddess *Sky Woman*, for instance, who was pushed down a hole by her jealous husband, owed her life to birds that carried her down to earth safely and then assisted her in the creation of the earth. In all Pueblo emergence accounts, a plant that grew high enough and a badger that dared to climb up and push a hole through the crust of the earth, enabled the people to reach the next world and complete their creative design. In the Navaho Legends recorded towards the end of the nineteenth century, Matthews writes: "It is difficult for such a people to conceive of a Supreme God. Their gods, like their men, stand much on a level of equality."[8]

The inability of most westerners to understand and/or accept the differing spiritual concepts of Native America led to immense mythological transformations which severely affected the tribes' social structure. Christianized versions often replaced traditional accounts of mythic events. A Hopi story, for instance, features a male fertility god who is referred to as "the virgin of the earth."[9] Allen points out that in many instances the primacy of a female creator was replaced by male gods: "Among the Cherokee, the goddess of the river foam is easily replaced by Thunder in many tales, and the Iroquois divinity Sky Woman now gets her ideas and powers from her dead father or her monstrous grandson." This reformation of traditional tribal versions of history, mythology, and the oral tradition, "increases the likelihood that the patriarchal non-Indians and patriarchalized Indians, will be incorporated into the spiritual and popular traditions of the tribes." This tendency, Allen continues, "is reinforced by the loss of rituals, medicine societies, and entire clans through assimilation and a dying off of tribal members familiar with the elder rituals and practices."[10]

As opposed to the usage of "symbol" in the western sense--as a representation concealing another meaning or some independent reality--a mythical symbol in the Native American sense implies a (momentary) identification with the essence and the reality of the object. Thus, mythical thinking "uses symbolic representations but without differentiating the symbols from their objects."[11] Similarly, among southwestern tribes, like among other Native American cultures, words have a special power that is integral to their sound. Words create what they signify, that is, language creates reality. The word "shipap," the hole in the center of the Kiva, does not just represent "shipap," the Place-of-Emergence, but **is** that place through which people from the lower worlds emerged into upper spheres. The recitation of a myth of creation, by the same token, is understood to be an actual, not a symbolic, recapitulation of that primordial creative process or event. "It does not say so much 'this happened long ago'," Frye maintains, "as 'what you are about to see, or have just seen, *is* what happened long ago!'"[12] Similarly, when Silko's Ceremony begins by saying that the stories are the only way "to fight off illness and death" (C 2), it is to be taken verbatim. Tribal reality is the cyclical, non-linear continuance of the stories' wisdom and order which are necessary to heal a world out of balance. Any reader of Native American literature has to realize "that the stories and reality in the novel are one."[13] Momaday goes even further, suggesting that existence is dependent upon language. He writes that the "state of human *being* is an idea . . . which man has of himself. Only when he is embodied in an idea, and the idea is realized in language," he continues, "can man take possession of himself."[14]

Furthermore, "no word exists alone," the narrator in Ceremony states, "and the reason for choosing each word had to be explained with a story about why it must be said this certain way" (C 35). In House Made of Dawn, the priest Tosamah emphasizes the Native Americans' perception of words as opposed to the western concept of spoken language:

> The white man takes such things as words and literature for granted. . . . He has diluted and multiplied the Word, and words have begun to close in upon him. He is sated and insensitive; his regard for language - for the Word itself - as an instrument of creation has diminished nearly to the point of no return. It may be that he will perish by the Word (HMD 89).

Even in contemporary Native American literature, words are not understood in the current western literary (postmodernist) sense--as parodies of myths, history, and reality, satiric and utopian word games, or playful artefacts--but are taken seriously and are pronounced with great care. Words have meaning in themselves and are needed to attain certain goals such as health, rain, and fertility. The protagonists in all four novels, for example, are healed through a careful reiteration of ritualistic or traditional texts. Words, even names and thoughts, have the power to create and thus serve a very distinct function. Names, as Lame Deer says, also convey great power. "Not Charles, Dick and George," but "Red Cloud, Black Elk, Whirlwind, Two Moons, Lame Deer - these names have a relationship to the Great Spirit." Each name has a story behind it, a vision, and a quest for dreams. "We receive great gifts from the source of a name; it links us to nature, to the animal nations. It gives power. You can lean on a name, get strength from it."[15] In the course of his transformation from an emotionally unstable person to a well-balanced human being, Set, the protagonist of Momaday's The Ancient Child, will discover for himself the immense power names hold in a tribal context.

In his influential essay, "The Man Made of Words," Momaday further emphasizes the importance of language. He relates the story of an arrowmaker who sat inside a tipi with his wife, straightening arrows in his mouth. Suddenly he noticed a stranger looking inside from the darkness. In Kiowa, his native tongue, the arrowmaker said casually that the stranger should give his name. When the person outside remained silent, the arrowmaker pointed in all directions with his arrow and then killed the stranger with a single shot.[16] The words used to determine the identity of his unannounced visitor serves as a protective "shield" the arrowmaker lifted up to protect the lives of his family. Thus, words were indeed his means of survival. Momaday gives another impressive example of the immediacy of words when he relates his meeting with Ko-sahn. One night while sitting at his desk he pronounced the name of his grandmother:

> Then it was that ancient, one-eyed woman Ko-sahn stepped out of the language and stood before me on the page. I was amazed. Yet it seemed to me entirely appropriate that this should happen. "I was just now writing about you," I replied, stammering. "I thought - forgive me - I thought that perhaps you were. . . ." "No," she said. And she cackled, I thought. And she went on. "You have imagined me well, and so I am. You have imagined that I dream, and so I do. I have seen the falling stars." "But all of this, this imagining," I protested, "this has taken place - is taking place in my mind. You are not actually here, not here in this room." It occurred to me that I was being extremely rude, but I could not help myself. She seemed to understand. "Be careful of your pronouncements, grandson," she answered. "You imagine that I am here in this room, do you not? That is worth something. You see, I have existence, whole being, in your imagination. It is but one kind of being, to be sure, but it is perhaps the best of all kinds. If I am not here in this room, grandson, then surely neither are you."[17]

A similar mode of understanding, paralleling that of language, is found in the way Native Americans of the Southwest perceive their arts and crafts. The natural materials used in any creative activity possess sacred powers due to their manifestations as the generative forces of the earth. In <u>House Made of Dawn</u>, Abel, inarticulate and no longer attuned to the natural rhythm of his environment, resents his inability to partake in creation:

> He was alone, and he wanted to make a song out of the colored canyon, the way the women of Torreón made songs upon their looms out of colored yarn, but he had not got the right words together. It would have been a creation song; he would have sung lowly of the first world, of fire and flood, and of the emergence of dawn from the hills (HMD 57).[18]

The completed form itself, or what is externally represented, manifests its own sacred power. There is no separation between the created form and the message or power this form bears and transmits. The circular design created by women on southwestern baskets, for example, is a representation of "shipap," the Place-of-Emergence, and thus the artistic recapitulation of the total process of creation. "The completed basket is the universe in an image," Brown maintains, "and in the manufacturing process the woman actually plays the part of the Creator."[19] The design directly connects the events of creation, regardless of time and space, with contemporary existence. Thus, man-made items embody the same significance as natural phenomena, and as such replicate the most fundamental truths of the origin stories as preserved in the oral tradition.

ii.

oral tradition

> The oral tradition is that process by which the myths, legends, tales, and lore of a people are formulated, communicated, and preserved in language by word of mouth, as opposed to writing.[1]

The force of Native American literature of the Southwest can be traced to its recognizable emergence from the realm of mythology--not mythology of a long forgotten past, but the current and viable myths of "time immemorial." The "rich mythic accounts of creation," writes Brown, "are not so much of chronological time-past as they usually tend to be read by us. Rather they tell of processes which are of eternal happening; the same processes are recurring now and are to recur in other cycles."[2]

Evaluating the remarkable strength of the oral tradition to survive different narrators, different audiences, and different centuries, Blumenberg points to the 'selective ability of the oral tradition', that is, its temporal resistence and stability. These characteristics result both from the compelling need of non-literary cultures to keep the most significant and the emotionally most disturbing structural and thematic narrative elements alive and strong, and from orality's non-reliance on history. Since the creation stories are never located at a specific point in time, non-literary cultures know no historical precision. Significance and meaningfulness, especially in a socio-cultural context, therefore assume the main role in oral narratives.[3]

Since colonization and conquest set the background to the confrontation between literate and non-literate peoples, the responses of Euro- and Native Americans to the cultural "Other" have been in the context of oppression and destruction. In a cultural context these political facts--which naturally affected the entire range of encounters--resulted in the literary irreverence towards oral accounts. The aura of inferiority even prevails where attempts have been made to substitute written accounts for oral narratives:

> The outward appearance of a printed collection of oral narratives immediately gives away a basic feature of our attitude toward such narratives: we regard them as a sort of primitive or nonliterate counterpart to our own written prose fiction and thus set them forth in gray masses of words broken only by paragraphing, labeled with words (myth, tale, or legend) that imply something other than plain truth.[4]

The forms and elements organic to Native American literature--all of which are intimately tied to an ongoing oral tradition--are at first glance deceptively simple. And it is this apparent simplicity that first poses a challenge to those used to purely formalist paradigms. The repetition of words, phrases, lines, as well as the constant reiteration of entire concepts and ideas, initially suggest a narrative structure below the complex level of Euro-American literature. This structure, however, not only replicates but embodies native philosophical concepts, such as the circularity of the universe and the identity of narrative and actual time. Other specific qualities of Native American literature include the simultaneity of different narrative levels and the representation of the numinous aspects of nature. Emphasizing the linearity of time and the horizontal rather than vertical (climactic) chain of events, the mythical, historical, and immediate narrative voices in written literature validate, according to Momaday, "the oral tradition to an extent that might not otherwise be possible."[5] These different narrative levels might reside side by side (as in Silko's Ceremony and Momaday's The Ancient Child), easily recognizable for even the most unsuspecting reader, or be intertwined (as in Momaday's House Made of Dawn). Through symbolic implication, both levels constantly influence each other in either case. In an attempt to replicate the numinous nature of the universe--a feature prevalent in oral accounts--people, animals, and (natural) objects contain numinous attributes. This elaborate, interconnected code of numinous mythical symbols creates meaning above the inherent significance of individual symbolic elements.

Why, one might ask, have these features bound to an ongoing oral tradition, yet seemingly out of sink with mainstream literary expression, survived until today, and are currently enjoying a revival in contemporary native literature? The aspect of 'function' becomes significant in this context: by supplying a specifically Native American worldview, and thus connecting a native audience through the shared knowledge of traditional themes, common characters, and familiar situations, contemporary Native American literature (like the oral accounts centuries earlier) excludes an audience unwilling to delve into a Native American framework. It thus functions not only as a bond between tribal members, but also as a means of resistance to an overpowering "ideological domination."[6]

Due to the political and cultural repression of southwestern tribes, there exists great resistance among the people to have their oral accounts written down. Concerning his research on the Navajo creation story, Zolbrod comments on the difficulties of convincing tribal people to help transform oral accounts into written texts:

> If I did not fully appreciate that complexity when I began this work, I came to realize it as I asked various Navajos for help. While most of them cooperated, many were hostile to the idea of having it written down. More than once I was told that if the old culture was indeed dying out the traditional stories should die with it. Some complained that print was an undesirable medium for stories that should properly be recited; words on a page were silent and unalive (Dinė 21-22).

The Navajo believe "that the life and power of their mythology depends upon its being retained in the memory of the people," Gill states, "and that to record the mythology is . . . to take away its vitality."[7] The Pueblos, too, are suspicious of the process of transforming oral literature into written accounts. "Among the Pueblo people," says Silko, "a written speech or statement is highly suspect because the true feelings of the speaker remain hidden as he reads words that are detached from the occasion and the audience."[8] To transform oral literature into writing is extremely difficult and, as Silko in Storyteller points out, potentially dangerous:

> [Nora's] grandchildren had brought home / a . . . book that had / my 'Laguna Coyote' poem in it./ [She said:] 'We all enjoyed it so much / But I was telling the children / the way my grandpa used to tell it / is longer.' / 'Yes, that's the trouble with / writing,' I said. / 'You can't go on and on the way / we do when we tell stories / around here.'[9]

However, out of the difficulties that arise in the attempt to transform oral literature, Silko creates a new poem. She advances the oral tradition by using written words, thereby creating a hybrid form of literary expression. By combining western literary components with oral accounts, Silko retains native traditions both despite and because of the adaptation of western elements. She thereby adopts the southwestern survivor attitude of the past centuries--the selection of desirable elements from the dominant culture and their subsequent incorporation into native culture--to suit her literary creations.

There exist, however, other voices. In her critique of Ceremony, Allen reiterates the danger involved in transforming oral into written accounts. The story Silko "lays alongside the novel," Allen writes,

> is a clan story and is not to be told outside of the clan. I have long wondered why she did so. Certainly, being raised in greater proximity to Laguna village than I, she must have been told what I was, that we don't tell these things outside. Perhaps her desire to

> demonstrate the importance of breeds led her to do this, or perhaps no one ever told her why the Lagunas and other Pueblos are so closed about their spiritual activities and the allied oral tradition.[10]

What Allen criticizes here is the exact and complete disclosure--without even slight alterations--of a sacred story considered spiritual property of a specific clan or community. While Silko's reasons for incorporating a "real" story is of no concern in the context of this chapter, it nevertheless remains questionable whether complete, or near complete, authenticity is even possible within the confines of written literature. Is it not, as a matter of fact, likely that the sacredness of a story already disappears through the mere act of writing? Considering the multitude of elements that necessarily vanish in the process of transforming oral accounts into written works (i.e. stress and rhythm patterns, breathing, pausing) the question remains whether it is even possible to achieve the same degree of "sacredness" on a printed page, or whether "sacredness" in a Native American context is necessarily bound to oral discourse.

Notwithstanding the negative aura that surrounds printed materials reminiscent of oral literature, Allen, Momaday, and Silko employ the myths preserved in the oral tradition for theme and structure. Thus they lend support to Branislaw Malinowski's perception that a myth is "not an idle tale, but a hard-working active force."[11] Legends--the narratives generated by myths--and rituals and ceremonies--the enactment of those legends--ensure the vitality and renewal of the mythic characters and events. They secure both the preservation and continuation of the traditional narratives as well as the spiritual existence of tribal life:

> Ritual can be defined as a procedure whose purpose is to transform someone or something from one condition or state to another. . . . Thus a healing ritual changes a person from an isolated (diseased) state to one of incorporation (health); a solstice ritual turns the sun

> path from a northerly direction to a southerly or vice versa; a hunting ritual turns the hunted animal's thoughts away from the individuals consciousness of physical life to total immersion in collective consciousness. . . . In the transformation from one state to another, the prior state or condition must cease to exist. It must die.[12]

Ritual based cultures are founded on the assumption that the universe is aware and alive. Through their traditional ceremonies, Native Americans recognize both the significance of life and find a way to maintain the perfect balance and order that was given to the world in the beginning. "In this view," Gill maintains, "their ritual acts are creative acts of the highest order, since the object of their creation is the world itself."[13] Centered on Native American themes and grounded in the ritualistic and mythic tradition of their respective tribes, Allen, Momaday, and Silko adapt ritual narrative structures to convey meaning. They thereby succeed in re-creating and renewing the ancient relationship that exists between contemporary man and the people and events of the origin stories.

iii.

reality and mythology

> The story of origin serves at once as a prototype for a ceremonial performance and as a wellspring of philosophy and world view. A distinctive characteristic of this paradigm is the way in which it unifies the primordial and physical geographies, the ethereal and the commonplace, the spiritual and the material.[1]

"The Origin story," says Silko, "functions basically as a maker of our identity - with the story we know who we are."[2] What is true for the Pueblos holds equal significance and validity for the Navajo tribe. Zolbrod writes: "In my research I encountered a direct relationship between the elements of Navajo poetic tradition and the way Navajos conduct their daily lives. The separateness of art that marks our own culture simply does not apply in Navajo culture." In the course of his research Zolbrod became aware of how much the Navajo creation story "gives individual Navajos . . . an important ethnic identity" (Dinė 25).[3]

According to southwestern belief the universe contains two major groups "who are related through proximity and symbiotic, reciprocal relationships: Earth Surface People (ordinary humans, both living and dead), and Holy People."[4] There is no distinct separation between the Earth People and the Holy People: some southwestern supernaturals and gods/goddesses are timeless, sacred figures who are ever present, while others are mortal beings with the ability to take on sacred functions. The Holy People of the Navajos, for instance, may have "human forms or they may be anthropomorphized animals, plants, natural phenomena, or even material objects."[5] All Earth Surface People, in turn, have their divine ancestral prototype and may assume mythic proportions. Due to this interchangeability, the transcendence which characterizes western divinities is replaced by a sense of immanence in the mythological figures of the Southwest. All this attests to the very direct relationship between religion, narrative, and everyday life in Navajo and Pueblo cultures. Listening to the creation stories and chantways is "by no means mere entertainment," but also "an act of sharing knowledge wherein art and learning cannot be separated" (Diné 355).

Origin stories are part of the religious tradition of every tribe and are central to the position of women in Native American communities. The vigor exhibited by the mythic women-figures in creation stories and related chants has been reflected historically in the position of women within tribal societies. Whereas the creation myths of northeastern and eastern tribes have undergone drastic changes, the southwestern myths display a remarkable continuity with respect to the stability of female divinities. There are various reasons why the mythical image of women--and thus their real-life significance--did not diminish to the same extent in the Southwest as it did elsewhere. Due to a vast landscape with seemingly little to offer, settlers, missionaries, and government agencies showed initially less interest (which translated quite simply into fewer whites and less dominion) in the arid southwestern area. Second, the southwestern tribes either have been or have become sedentary peoples. They are dependent on the control of their natural habitat and follow therefore a strict and deeply entrenched ceremonial system based on the cycles of nature. These ceremonies connect the members of each tribe ritually, making them less vulnerable to outside pressures. Unwilling to abandon a religious system which had always provided the necessities of life, the tribes of the Southwest either integrated foreign elements into their ceremonial order, or maintained their own traditions while superficially adapting to foreign social and religious standards. Due to the above reasons, the origin stories of the Pueblos, which the Navajos adopted and built on, did not undergo the same alterations that occurred in many northeastern legends. As a result, the vigorous and responsible woman-figure featured in the creation myths and the related chantways still integrates the female as a powerful force into southwestern society.

A Native American woman is primarily defined by her tribal identity. But in no tribal definition is she perceived in the same way as women in western industrial and postindustrial cultures:

> Among Christians, the madonna is the female prototype, and she is portrayed as essentially passive: her contribution is simply that of birthing . . . and she certainly possesses few of the characteristics that are attributed to mythic figures among Indian tribes.

Instead of balancing this image of the female in western societies, it is countered, Allen continues, by both the "witch-goddess/whore characteristics designed to reinforce cultural beliefs about women, as well as western adversarial and dualistic perceptions of reality."[6] As opposed to contemporary Greco-Roman mythologies or the western creation story, the Bible, the role of southwestern goddesses is indeed striking: they do not function as helpmates of an all-powerful male deity, but **created** the universe, and/or people, animals, and landscapes. *Thought Woman* of the Keres, for instance, conceived the earth and the original plan of creation; the Navajo's *Changing Woman* created mankind from the skin of her own body.

In Navajo and Pueblo society, both of which are matrilineal and matrilocal, women have always enjoyed authority and status, a fact reflected throughout the creation cycle. All **original** Pueblo creators as well as the most revered goddess of the Navajo, *Changing Woman*, are females.[7] Like her Pueblo counterparts, the Navajo goddess *Changing Woman* is the sole creator of human beings; unlike the Pueblo goddesses, however, she at last entered into an egalitarian relationship with *Sun*, her "husband":

> Remember, as different as we are, you and I, we are of one spirit. As dissimilar as we are, you and I, we are of equal worth. As unlike as you and I are, there must always be solidarity between the two of

us. Unlike each other as you and I are, there can be no harmony in the universe as long as there is no harmony between us (Dinė 275).

This relationship is crucial to the main theme of the Navajo creation story. Until *Changing Woman*'s demands to *Sun* could be met, "five-fingered Earth Surface People" could not exist in the uppermost, the Fifth World. Zolbrod suggests that "this precarious but necessary balance to be achieved between Changing Woman and the Sun is analogous to the harmony or balance that is to be achieved between the Earth Surface People and the gods, between man and animals, and between all of the disparate elements of the cosmos" (Dinė 405). Full harmony could not be established until *Changing Woman* and *Sun* achieved a relationship based on equal rights and responsibilities. Everything that happens throughout the creation story relates directly or indirectly to the notion of the perfect balance between male and female.

Location, rather than language, is the decisive factor in linking primal cultures mythologically. By sharing the same geographical environment, the Pueblos and their Athabascan neighbors also share a common cosmology.[8] One distinct difference between the Pueblo and the Navajo world view, however, is the significance of the individual. Although the Navajos took possession of the basic structure of Pueblo ceremonialism, they never adopted the Pueblo system of subordinating individual desires to the demands of tribal well-being. The Navajo healing ceremonies are centrifugal, concerned foremost with the "balancing" (healing) of the individual. The healthiness of the restored person, then, radiates outward, ultimately ensuring the well-being of the entire tribe. Despite some differences in the social, political, and ceremonial organizations of the Navajo and Pueblo tribes, it is nevertheless possible "to suggest certain generalizations if the differences are understood to be dialects of a commonly shared cosmological and spiritual language."[9]

The resemblance between the opening of the Navajo creation story and its allied Pueblo narratives suggests that together with the agriculture they acquired from the Pueblos, the Navajos also assumed ownership of the accompanying creation stories, adapting them to their own indigenous myths and rituals. By confronting Pueblo cosmology, "the world view which has been taking shape in the Southwest for about two thousand years," the Navajos' Athabascan hunting traditions eventually harmonized with Pueblo ceremonialism. "All this together, in the course of a few centuries," he claims, "produced a ceremonial ferment which is unequaled anywhere in North America."[10] Due to the above reasons, and because the Navajo myth presents a more unified account than the diverse Pueblo narratives, I will focus on the Navajo creation myth and contrast it--wherever appropriate--with the relevant Pueblo versions.

In their emergence accounts neither the Navajos nor the Pueblos are concerned with any historical explanations as to the exact origin of their tribes. As opposed to the Bible, which focuses on an absolute point in time, marking both the most significant religious event and the beginning of modern chronology, myth is never located within a time frame. By insisting on a definite chronology, Christianity is of course highly susceptible to charges of "ahistoricalness" and finds it increasingly difficult to fit the dates of biblical creation into the framework of emerging scientific findings. Free of the strictures of chronological developments, tribal mythic accounts instead emphasize the function of myth to set rules and stabilize roles of behavior.[11]

"The emergence of mankind," as Tyler explains, "is not a creation, but a bringing forth of people who already existed, though sometimes in an imperfect state." Not so much physical confusion, but social disorder was the reason for the emergence to an upper world. Constant fighting and quarreling between men and women forced an abduction of the old sphere and a reaching towards a higher level. The Pueblo and Navajo emergence myths not only point toward an evolution of the biological and social order, but even more toward "the order that attends the religious and ceremonial functioning of . .

. society."[12] The emergence myths, the foundation of Navajo and Pueblo philosophy, establish certain principles clearly:

> The world is a cyclical ordered, living reality of fragile relationships among intelligent, volitional beings, to whom man is intimately related through his prior forms and history.
>
> All things are complementary. Nothing is whole or sufficient in itself. Mind, body, and spirit are interrelated.
>
> Man's role is actively to maintain harmony and integration among the elements of creation through ritual.
>
> Control, order, is good; lack of control, disorder, is not.
>
> The world is dangerous because nature is more powerful than man, but is not necessarily feared because power is available for all contingencies.
>
> "Sin" and illness are disorders; disorder does not accrue guilt; it requires only repair.[13]
>
> Like produces like, and the part stands for the whole; this is the best of all possible worlds; it is this life that counts.
>
> Nothing is ever lost; there is an economy even in dying.[14]

One purpose of the emergence myths is to display the system of interdependent relationships which gives basic structure to the universe. Within this highly integrated system symbolic associations are attached to a variety of elements--including animal and plant species, minerals, colors, directions, seasons and other meteorologic phenomena and topographic features. "The whole story," Zolbrod maintains, "occurs in a setting that combines the real and the earthy with the mystical and the cosmic, where spirits and humans interact in a way not duplicated in any one of our own familiar literary works . . ." (Dinė 6).[15]

The relationship between human and non-human--as it applies to Navajo and Pueblo storytelling and ceremonial tradition--is explained by Luckert who introduces the term "prehuman flux." That term "refers to man's primeval kinship with all creatures of the living world and to the essential continuity among them all."[16]

> Navajo gods still today participate in the mythological stratum of prehuman flux - they are not restricted to certain anthropomorphic, theriomorphic, or occupational manifestations; they can equally well hide and show themselves in the shimmering lights of dawn, midday, and sunset; total invisibility is also in their power.[17]

As in most Pueblo accounts, the Navajos emerged from four underworlds into the present Fifth World. The First World, identified by the color "red," was "small and barren." The Second, the "blue," World was "dry and cheerless." The Third World "was yellow and barren, but had a river flowing through it toward the east." The Fourth World, finally, "resembled the others but was larger; the couriers took four days to return from their survey of it."[18]

Not able to either call in good from the outside or to drive out evil, the Navajos had to move themselves to an uncontaminated environment which eventually culminated in their emergence to the present world. Through ceremonies this set of underworlds, described by Zolbrod as "the loci of a flawed collective past" (Dinė 351), has to be subliminally relived and corrected. Similar to the Hopi emergence account, these series of movements from chaos to order represent an evolution towards greater social harmony and a more uniform symbolic arrangement. Progress is solely measured by intellectual criteria:

> In characterizing their forebears the Navaho ascribe to them sentience and a cognizance of human problems. . . . The wanderers had no social institutions and had to learn to recognize them among the people into whose territory they intruded. As they were addicted to sorcery, they were antisocial; they offended strangers by wife-stealing and other sexual offenses. However, upon arriving in a new world the primordial ancestors of the Navaho made vows to co-operate with the natives; as they learned more and more they kept their promises longer and longer. At each pause in the upward migration they accepted more social curbs - some were learned from the old residents, some were commands of their own leaders. . . . Each subsequent step in the emergence changed the emphasis until now, in this world, stability, knowledge, and co-operation are ideals, the chrysalis of ignorance having been shed in the lower worlds.[19]

The pattern of the emergence narrative--a journey towards order--is repeated in Navajo healing ceremonies, like the Mountain Chant or the Night Chant. A patient requires a healing ceremony (or chantway ritual) when his life is in some way out of balance or harmony due, for instance, to illness, bad thoughts, or witchcraft. In order for harmony to be restored the patient must be taken through a symbolic re-emergence journey paralleling that of the Dinė (the [Navajo] People).[20] The creation story is thus fundamental to the entire array of healing ceremonies.

The people's increase in knowledge and social awareness is accompanied by an elaborate code of symbols. The cloud pillars of the First World, originally defined only by color and direction, eventually became the sacred mountains of the four directions in the Fifth World. The symbolic value of colors basic to Navajo ceremonialism is traditionally associated with the creation of the four sacred mountains marking the four cardinal points in the Fifth World. "White," a male color, stands for dawn; "blue," a female color, stands for broad daylight; "yellow," also female, is the evening twilight; and "black," a male color, is the darkness of night. The four corners of the Pueblo world also feature large mountain peaks, each of which houses a spirit or a god/goddess. Whereas the Pueblos with their separate centers had a hard time classifying those mountains, the Navajos who adopted this system, found it quite simple to identify the mountains with prominent peaks on the physical landscape. Created by *First Man* and *First Woman*, these mountains become the most important coordinates in an intricate mythological framework:[21]

> In the east they made *Sisnaajinł*, or Sierra Blanca Peak as *Bilagáana* [the white man] now calls it. In the south they made *Tsoodzil*, or Mount Taylor. In the west they made *Dook'o'oosłííd*, or San Francisco Peak as it is now called. And in the north they fashioned *Dibé nitsas*, or Big Mountain Sheep (Diné 86).

As in various Pueblo accounts, the Navajo world was not created by some powerful god, but through the powers of thought, song, and prayer. Personified prior to the creation of the world, song and prayer, or speech, arose from the medicine bundle, the source of all creation, in the form of a young man and woman. Their names are often rendered in English as *Long Life Boy* (thought), and *Happiness Girl* (speech).[22] "Speech," according to Zolbrod, represents "the highest human faculty in the Navajo hierarchy . . ." (Diné 13). The motif of pairing which runs through the entire creation cycle starts with "long life" and "happiness," then continues with *First Man* and *First Woman*, and finally culminates in the reconciliation of *Jóhonaa'éí*, *Sun*, and *Asdzáá nádleehé*, *Changing Woman*.

In the Navajo version of the creation story, male and female supernatural beings, (like the *First Pair*), were created by the Holy People (although they are divided into male and female this division represents a distinction of power only) under the prime supervision of *Talking God.* Male and female supernaturals were created simultaneously, and each was endowed with peculiar qualities and made dependent upon the other for existence. In turn, the supernatural beings "created" the female goddess, *Changing Woman*, who owes her name to her remarkable ability to grow older through time, reach old age, and repeat the cycle of life again and again. She is thus associated with the continual and eternal process of life itself. The bundle she received from *First Man* was the source of her own existence, since her "parents," *First Man* and *First Woman*, and/or *Long Life Boy* and *Happiness Girl*, personify the powers it holds.

In Pueblo origin accounts the female goddess was simply "there," with no explanation given as to how she came into being, and "created," that is, thought or breathed life into people. The Navajo's *Changing Woman*, on the other hand, after being "created" from ears of corn, got magically impregnated and gave **actual** birth to twin boys. The first-born, *Monster-Slayer*, rid the world of monsters, the second, *Born-of-Water*, is parent of all the waters of the world.[23] After giving birth to the culture heroes, *Changing Woman* created beings like herself (Earth Surface People, the ancestors of the Navajos) from the rubbings of her skin on her back, her breasts, and her shoulders. Then she used her creative powers to make the earth ready and suitable for the newly created race. Only after both *Monster-Slayer* and *Born-of-Water* were grown did *Changing Woman* willingly enter into a relationship with *Sun.* While she and other supernaturals eventually parted, they are nevertheless considered to be "ever present as anthropomorphic inner forms of various natural phenomena and forces [and] because of a Messenger Wind communication network, all-knowing and -overseeing."[24] Since movement and change in the Navajo creation myth emanate from women, Witherspoon, in accordance with Fr. Berard Haile, identifies the dichotomy of male (static) and female (active), and observes that it is the active, restless female whose impulses are to create.[25]

In passing on to her people the knowledge of Blessingway -based on the myth of her own rejuvenating abilities--*Changing Woman* charged the Navajos with the responsibility of maintaining the world in its state of perfect balance and beauty. She warned them never to forget the Blessingway songs for Navajo life depends upon them:

> In the view of native ritualists, Blessingway . . . 'controls' the entire ceremonial system. That is, each ceremonial must include at least one Blessingway song in order to sanctify it - which lends support to the observation made repeatedly by outsiders that Changing Woman is the central deity of Navajo religion.[26]

The basic theme of the Navajo creation story is the solidarity between men and women, a solidarity necessary to keep the universe in harmony. In comparison to the Navajo acceptance of opposites, the Pueblo myths constantly depict alternatives to reconcile differences, often with the use of humor. Both in content and in form the Navajo and Pueblo creation stories glorify not conflict and disruption, but the order and harmony achieved as a result of it.

In both the Pueblo and Navajo creation stories female goddesses were clearly present before any male deities. The concept propagated in the Old Testament that woman was made from man which forms the basis of traditional occidental religious thought, is not found in Native American religion. Instead, women of southwestern tribes to this day derive great strength from their mythic import as creators of the world, and they continue to play significant roles in the lives and the literatures of the people they represent. The remarkable continuity between the strong and powerful women in creation stories of the Southwest and the women characters in modern Native American literature will be examined below.

In order to assess the importance of women-figures in native literature of the Southwest, a closer analysis of their mythological prototypes is invaluable. In the context of the literary works under discussion, I will therefore delineate the sacred creator-goddesses of the Southwest more closely and outline some of the functions they exercise within the myth cycles of their respective cultural settings. The exploration of these goddesses and the symbols that surround them will, in turn, reveal and illuminate the mythic characteristics of both female and male figures in contemporary Native American literature of the Southwest.

IV. Mythological Women in Contemporary Literature

i.
introductory remarks

> [The] structure of Pueblo expression resembles something like a spider's web - with many little threads radiating from a center, criss-crossing each other. As with the web, the structure will emerge as it is made and you must simply listen and trust, as the Pueblo people do, that meaning will be made.[1]

The novels by Allen, Momaday, and Silko feature themes that characterize and define Native American life in Native American terms. The narratives concern people, themes, and symbols derived from traditional mythologies. In the spirit of Pueblo oral tradition which is essentially anonymous since the author either "has heard it from an elder or [has] received it from a supernatural power," Allen and Silko do not consider themselves the "originator of [their] material but merely the conveyor." Pueblo literature, Bierhorst continues, is thus "usually attributed not to an individual but to [a] culture."[2] Momaday, on the other hand, being grounded in the more individualistic philosophy of Navajo belief, takes full authorial credit for his literary creations. All three novelists, aware of their oral-literary heritage and its implications for their own written narratives, either place their stories into a mythic framework or attribute them to a mythic persona.

A tribal member's estrangement from the web of tribal being (reservation life itself, and/or tribal stories and mythologies), and the conflict that arises from that separation are the central themes of the four novels to be discussed. For Momaday, Silko, and Allen, belonging is a basic assumption in these novels; alienation, on the other hand, is considered an abnormal state that can be corrected only through the restoration of the estranged to his or her place within the cultural matrix. The movement toward integration of the individual into the community, however, is accompanied by pain, rage, and powerlessness.

As opposed to the "leaving" plots of adventure books and novels of development, which assert that the protagonists' departure for better opportunities and more exotic places is the sole avenue towards achieving strength of character and personal integrity, the aspect most important in the novels of Allen, Momaday, and Silko is not the departure, but the return, of the protagonists. Coming home to one's heritage (physically and/or emotionally) is the most desirable goal. "These novels are important, not only because they depict Indian individuals coming home while white individuals are leaving but also because they suggest - variously and subtly and by degree - a tribal rather than an individual definition of 'being.'"[3] Home is not simply a place, but signifies the person's tribal belonging. As such, going home means finding one's self within the context of Native American values and traditions. In all four novels under consideration the protagonist returns emotionally and spiritually to where he or she came from (excepting Allen's novel the protagonists even return physically).

Each novel tells of a wanderer coming home. Although all four "home-comings" are different in nature, each of the protagonists returns to tribal values and beliefs. In Momaday's House Made of Dawn, a serviceman comes back to the reservation, yet finds himself unable to fit into tribal reality. After murdering a man and serving time, he finally returns to the Pueblo with the help of a Navajo friend. In what seems to be a rather sudden change of mind, but is in fact an emotional transformation instigated by a white woman he had met before on the reservation, Abel returns to the age-old rituals of his tribe. In The Ancient Child, a famous painter of Native American heritage who has established himself in white, main-stream America, experiences bouts of emotional instability after visiting the land of his forefathers. With the assistance of a young Navajo medicine woman he gets intuned with his "bear" power, his ancient, his "real" self. In Leslie Marmon Silko's Ceremony, a Native American serviceman returns from the war to his Laguna tribe. After a period of physical and psychological difficulties, he breaks from a pattern of drinking and madness to participation in a healing ceremony initiated by an old medicine man and concluded by a young medicine woman. In Paula Gunn Allen's The Woman Who Owned the Shadows, a young Laguna woman finds the solution to her emotional instability and her identity as both a Native American and a woman in the legends and rituals of her tribe.

Due to the effects of colonization and/or (imagined) spiritual and personal wrongdoings, the novels' protagonists must deal with an attendant sense of loss of self. Through ritual which gives their individual lives shape and significance, each achieves a vision which is "a mark of maturity, a kind of rite of passage."[4] In each novel the protagonist seeks a meaningful relationship to the larger context of tribal existence and becomes a healthy person through accepted social rituals.

The essential connection among all four novels consists in the authors' use of mythic archetypes, thereby releasing the "symbols and structures shared in a deeply buried unconsciousness by a community of people."[5] Through the lavish distribution of numinous qualities onto a variety of symbols, the characters in each novel are surrounded by a mythic "buffer zone." The mythic focus does not illuminate the protagonists alone but is spread onto a considerable number of symbols. The equal importance thus bestowed onto other literary aspects serves as an explanation why--with the exception of The Woman Who Owned the Shadows--each novel features a rather passive protagonist. The mythical "envelope" not only keeps and protects the protagonists from an oftentimes hostile environment and functions as a decisive factor in the protagonists' attainment of health and well-being, it also emphasizes the paramount role of the so-called "secondary," the women-characters.

All four novels celebrate the connection between contemporary action and mythic event, between contemporary people and mythic prototypes. So far, the mythic role of the female characters which clarifies the mythic stature of the protagonists, has largely gone unnoticed. The role of the male protagonists will be reevaluated; the emphasis, however, will be placed on the women-figures in their mythic realm. Angela from House Made of Dawn, for example, will not only be shown as a person undeserving of her negative characterization, but as a mythic woman-figure essential to the protagonist's successful integration into tribal tradition.[6]

ii.

N. Scott Momaday[1]

Angela and First Woman

House Made of Dawn Revisited

> Yet [Angela] and Abel are able to relate to one another on one level. . . . So she enables us, I think, to see the pueblo world and Abel in [their] traditional context.[2]

Momaday has structured House Made of Dawn according to the main restorative performance to come out of the Navajo creation myth, the Night Chant. The Night Chant, which supersedes all other ceremonies, is commonly called *Ye'i bichai*, "Grandfather-of-the-gods," or "maternal Grandfather of the Ye'i," referring to *Talking God*, the leader of the ceremony. The Night Chant begins at sunset and ends with rebirth at sunrise eight and a half days later; it is a major winter curing ceremony that can be held only after the snakes and bears are asleep and there is no longer danger of lightning.[3] The historian Carl Gorman explains the Night Chant:

> In the most beautiful of our ceremonies, the Yei-Bi-Chei, or Nine-night chant, dancers, masked as personifications of the Holy People . . . are led by the Talk-God. . . . This is a healing ceremony of Blessingway and is being held at home at various places, through the winter months. . . . We believe in the duality of all things. Everything has its opposite, or its positive and negative side. We do not believe that evil can overcome good. Blessingway is more powerful than evil. The destructive forces unleashed by following a negative, selfish path are restored to harmony when man has the will to walk the path of beauty.[4]

"The Night Chant," writes Reichard, "and, possibly, the Mountain Chant, all of which have numerous subdivisions, belong to the category 'good.'"[5] Thus, the primary purpose of the Night Chant and its related rituals is the healing of the emotionally disturbed person, based on the Navajo understanding that health depends on an integrated psyche. In the Navajo system, an isolated or alienated individual is a sick one; the healing practice centers therefore on leading the isolated individual back into the matrix of the universe. The poetic language of the chants and prayers combine with symbolic action to form the healing power necessary to achieve psychic integration. Words are used to paint images and symbols and to evoke visual and imaginative responses in the minds of the participants. By multiplying the number of mental images the ceremony builds momentum. As verbal repetition intensifies, sound, imagery, and symbolic action all combine to create the stability and equilibrium necessary to achieve the desired outcome. The ceremonial method of the Night Chant is twofold; on the one hand, "the ritual repulses 'evil,' on the other it attracts 'holiness.' Accordingly, each of its separate rites may be categorized as either repulsive or attractive, as either purgative or additory."[6] Momaday's House Made of Dawn is an elaborate ceremony designed to heal. Like the Night Chant, it moves from sickness and disharmony to health and harmony, attributing utmost significance to all elements--animals, people, colors, directions--as essential to the participant's successful integration process.

Tosamah's evocation of his own tribal ancestry briefly introduces Kiowa culture; in all other aspects House Made of Dawn is mainly concerned with Navajo and Jemez Pueblo cultures. Momaday draws heavily on southwestern mythic tradition in which images and symbols function as part of the poetic processes of creation, transformation, and restoration. Since Abel personifies mythic heroes from both the Night Chant as well as the Mountainway, the meaning of his experience is not evident unless especially Navajo myths are taken into account. The combination of southwestern mythology is further exemplified in the character of Angela Grace Martin St. John who combines aspects of both Navajo and Pueblo supernaturals.

The Native American community in which Abel, the story's protagonist, grows up belongs to the Rio Grande Pueblos in New Mexico. Momaday opens the first chapter with the place name "Walatowa, Canyon de San Diego." Walatowa literally means "the people in the canyon," and is the native name of Jemez. The Prologue features Abel's participation in the winter race, the first race in the Jemez ceremonial season. It is an anticipation of the final scene, making the novel structurally and thematically cyclic and turning it into a complex, four-part flashback. On a symbolic level the novel parallels the Navajo emergence journey as described in the creation story. In an oftentimes painful ascent through the four lower worlds, the journey of the People, like that of Abel, also culminates in the safe arrival in the current, the Fifth World.

House Made of Dawn opens and closes with the traditional words which enclose all Jemez Pueblo tales--*dypaloh* and *qtsedaba*, placing it consciously within the framework of tribal myths. The mythic references in the first paragraph set the tone for the entire novel:

> There was a house made of dawn. It was made of pollen and rain, and the land was very old and everlasting. There were many colors on the hills, and the plain was bright with different-colored clays and sands. Red and blue and spotted horses grazed in the plain and there was a dark wilderness on the mountains beyond. The land was still and strong. It was beautiful all around (HMD 1).

The geographical area, the Southwest, is embedded in a mythic dimension by the description of the "red and blue and spotted horses" (HMD 7). The Pueblo color symbolism derived from the emergence story designates "red" as the sacred color of the south, and "blue" as the sacred color of the west. In addition, "red" and "blue" are the colors ascribed to the First and Second

World respectively. The beginning of the novel thus mirrors the early stages of the emergence into a better world.

Part 1, "The Longhair," is set at Jemez during the late summer 1945 and comprises six sections, each covering events of a specific day. Abel's childhood and early adult experiences are narrated in flash-back sequences. One of the first things we learn about Abel is that he "did not know who his father was" (HMD 15). The fact that his father is unknown makes him an outsider within the Pueblo social structure; it also relates him to two great Navajo heroes: first, to the main character of the Mountain Chant, grandson of *Older Sister*; and second, to *Monster-Slayer*, hero of the Navajo creation story, son of *Changing Woman.*[7] He and his brother, *Born-of-Water*, constantly question their mother about their seemingly non-existent father (Diné 188-189). Later, when *Sun* turns out to be their father, they need counsel and guidance to find him and to fulfill his strict requirements. In House Made of Dawn, Abel's grandfather takes Abel and his brother Vidal to a mountain top to teach them the course of the sun, to show them where they live, to tell them who they are:

> He made them stand just there, above the point of the low white rock, facing east. They could see the black mesa looming on the first light, and he told them there was the house of the sun. They must learn the whole contour of the black mesa. They must know it as they knew the shape of their hands, always and by heart. The sun rose up on the black mesa at a different place each day. It began there, at a point on the central slope, standing still for the solstice, and ranged all the days southward across the rise and fall of the long plateau, drawing closer by the measure of mornings and moons to the lee, and back again. They must know the long journey of the sun on the black mesa, how it rode in the seasons and the years, and they must live according to the sun appearing, for only then could they reckon where they were, where all things were, in time (HMD 177).

Abel's mythical connection to his counterpart from the creation story is confirmed by Reichard's remark that "one of the most difficult of the hero's tests, a formal requirement of his instruction, was to name every holy place on the earth as he looked upon the panorama from a great height."[8] Francisco teaches Abel and Vidal the requirements necessary for tribal belonging, just as *Nilch'i*, *Wind*, had taught *Monster-Slayer* and *Born-of-Water* the information necessary to pass *Jóhonaa'éí's*, (*Sun's*) test, thus preparing them for their mythic role as saviors of mankind. The parallels are striking:

> *Jóhonaa'éí* sat on the west side of the hole while the twins sat on the east side. . . . While they sat there, *Jóhonaa'éí* the Sun pointed down through the sky hole. "You must show me your home down there," he said. "Indicate to me where in the world below you and your people belong." The brothers looked down and scanned the landscape far beneath them. But truly they were so high they could distinguish nothing upon the surface of the earth. . . . But even as the twin spoke, *Nilch'i* the Wind was whispering into the ear of his brother, instructing him on how to recognize the sacred mountains, the great rivers, the special peaks and the familiar forests (Diné 213-214).

As a youth, Francisco was chosen by the supernaturals, an honor that was signaled by his completion of a perfect race. On that day he did everything perfectly, "and from then on had a voice in the clan and the next year he healed a child who had been sick from birth" (HMD 187). It is clear that Francisco has bear power, for he tracks a large bear, and it agrees to give him its life (HMD 178-184). Since the powers of the bear are transmitted to humans, the hunting of animals is considered a "ritual activity [in which] food and hides and all parts of the animal [are] understood to partake of this sacrificial act, and of the sacred power of the particular animal."[9]

"At Jemez," Tyler writes, "the bear killer also becomes a 'scalp-taker,'" a title which brings great esteem and ritual recognition. "Bears, along with eagles and lions," he continues, "belong to a special class of game, in that one who kills any of these is eligible to join the Warrior's society, just as though he had killed a man."[10] Francisco is also a favorite of the old Spanish priest, Fray Nicolas, who, as rumor has it, might be his father (HMD 184). When Francisco grows up, however, the old priest rejects him, noticing that Francisco is a "longhair," a man adhering to traditional Pueblo rituals.

The theme of witchcraft is introduced by Francisco who sleeps with the daughter of a witch. When their child is still-born, he abandons his lover. Since time in Native American thought is non-linear and eternal with no determined beginning or end, once an event has occurred its effects may be felt at any given point. Holding him responsible for his grandfather's behavior, Nicolàs *teah-whau,* "had screamed at [Abel] some unintelligible curse," (HMD 15). The magnitude of her witchcraft becomes apparent when both Abel's mother and brother die. From now on Abel has to bear the curse placed upon the family by his grandfather's unacceptable act. It is up to Abel to undergo a healing ceremony in order to appease the supernaturals; yet, his alcohol problem and his emotional instability (both partly remnants of his participation in World War II), make him a rather unlikely candidate for "herohood."

With his mother gone, Abel loses the most important link to his cultural and spiritual heritage. In addition, he no longer has any positive female guidance in his life. An exception is Fat Josie who had cured Abel from a backache when he was a child. She is the prototypical southwestern storyteller/mother/matron: "And the children huddled against her and laid their heads on her great brown arms" (HMD 106). After his brother Vidal dies, Abel visits Josie who "crossed her eyes and stuck out her tongue and danced around the kitchen on her huge bare feet . . . and her great haunches quivered and her broad shining face cracked in a wonderfully stupid, four-teeth missing grin, and all the while tears were streaming from her eyes" (HMD 107). Francisco, however, monopolizes his education and forbids Abel to find a substitute mother.

One of the novel's flashback sequences describes Abel witnessing the mating flight of two eagles. His observation of the eagles gains him the permission of the reputable Eagle Watcher Society to take part in an eagle hunt. Abel, exhilarated by the sight of the majestic birds, lays a trap and catches the female:

> She swung back with a great clamor of her wings and fell with fury on the bait. . . . His hands closed upon her legs and he drew her down with all his strength. For one instant only did she recoil, splashing her great wings down upon the beams and boughs -and she very nearly broke from his grasp; but then she was down in the darkness of the well, hooded, and she was still (HMD 24).

He returns to the other hunters who celebrate him in much the same way as Francisco was celebrated after his successful bear hunt. Yet, the power and the majesty of the captured eagle fills him with dread. Seeing the great bird "bound and helpless," Abel "took hold of its throat in the darkness and cut off its breath" (HMD 24-25). Instead of realizing the importance of his act for tribal tradition, Abel is sad and disgusted, unable to enjoy this honor. He does not understand that his respect for the animal can be reconciled with the act of depriving it of its freedom for the benefit of the community. This killing "is not a ritual act," as Schubnell points out, "but an act of rebellion against a tribal custom Abel cannot comprehend."[11] As opposed to his grandfather who proceeded strictly according to the code of honor which regulates the hunt, Abel, despite his knowledge of ancient traditions and customs, reacts emotionally rather than ritualistically. With the killing he did not just commit a "faux pas" but an evil act, since in southwestern tradition "evil is that which is ritualistically not under control."[12] It becomes apparent that even before

Abel went to fight the white man's war, he had lost all contact to his tribal heritage. The war only furthered his alienation.

On July 20, 1945, Francisco hurries from the fields to meet his grandson who returns home from World War II. Abel is drunk, stumbling off the bus into his arms. "The breeze was very faint, and it bore a scent of earth and grain; and for a moment everything was all right with him. He was at home" (HMD 32). Abel's initial feeling of belonging only lasts "for a moment." Unable to relate to tribal life and deprived of his immediate family, Abel, more than before, is a person desperately in need of supernatural intervention.

Further introduced in Part I are Father Olguin, the resident priest, and Angela Grace Martin St. John, a white woman from Los Angeles. At first glance, it is not necessarily clear how Angela, a wealthy doctor's wife from the big city, could to any significant degree participate in a mythic context that eventually transforms "Abel from a fragmented, isolated human being into a member of a supernatural brotherhood and from an alienated man into a spiritual participant in the cosmic being of the tribe."[13] Judging merely from the space Angela occupies in House Made of Dawn, she plays a rather insignificant role. She occurs twice in the novel: in the first chapter, "The Longhair," which takes place at Walatowa, and in the third chapter, "The Night Chanter," which plays in Los Angeles. In the sections that follow, I will show that Angela displays characteristics of *First Woman*, considered by most mythologists to be the adoptive mother of *Changing Woman*, the most revered goddess of the Navajo.

Due to her origin as an ear of corn, *First Woman* is initially a rather rudimentary draft of a figure endowed with supernatural qualities; she reaches her divine potential only after many social and personal errors. She symbolizes transformation into human, and eventually, into superhuman form. *First Woman* has "an inkling of what is good and some desire to bring it about, but because of ignorance [and] the absence of harmony, [she] move[s] back and forth between good and evil in a kind of experiment with the cosmos."[14] Eventually she acquires a distinct personality of her own and assumes proportions that can easily be associated with the quintessential human spirit. As she gains experience and wisdom she takes on god-like proportions: she accumulates powers that seem magical, and she finally envisions the destiny that lies ahead for the as yet uncreated human race. As will be shown in the chapter "The Night Chanter," Angela's vision concerning Abel--comparable to that of *First Woman* concerning the future of all that exists--forecasts a new and more positive destiny for the novel's protagonist.

Of special significance in the origin myth is the Fourth World, in which human life as we now know it was formally created. The Fourth World, home to *First Woman* and *First Man*, is of added importance in the context of House Made of Dawn, since the rites of the Night Chant commemorate and celebrate the events of the fourth world.

> Proceeding silently, the gods [Holy People; powerful and virtuous, not necessarily holy] laid one buckskin on the ground, careful that its head faced the west. Upon this skin they placed the two ears of corn, being just as careful that the tips of each pointed east. Over the corn they spread the other buckskin, making sure that its head faced east. Under the white ear they put the feather of a white eagle. And under the yellow ear they put the feather of a yellow eagle. Then they told the onlooking people [Insect People] to stand at a distance. So that the wind could enter. . . . And lo! the ears of corn had disappeared. In their place there lay a man and there lay a woman (Diné 50).

Although Angela's appearances are brief they nevertheless establish her mythic significance. In the first chapter Angela resembles her mythological counterpart, *First Woman*, in that she does not quite achieve the full potential of a goddess figure. Like *First Woman*, she merely touches upon it. In

Reichard's "Pantheon of Deities," the *First Pair* belongs to the category "Undependable Deities," because "meanness or the desire to do mischief is a large part of their makeup." Little more than a basic, germinating seed in the beginning, *First Woman*'s knowledge, writes Reichard, "was imperfect because incomplete." What she does possess, and what Angela possesses to the same degree, is "a notion of conscious creation [and the] ability to glimpse the future."[15]

The first feature that links Angela to the Native American community is her appearance. Although she is a white woman her features are those of a Native American woman. "Her hair was very long and dark, so that ordinarily it appeared to be black . . ." (HMD 30). That Angela contains mythic proportions becomes further apparent through the color, direction, and animal symbolism which surrounds her appearances throughout the novel. Father Olguin is the first to see Angela when she walks along the fence which "was overgrown with blue and violet morning glories" (HMD 29). The presence of the color "blue" which represents "the fructifying power of the earth, especially as demonstrated by the . . . plants,"[16] emphasizes Angela's mythic proportions. The nature of symbolism intensifies when it concerns clothing. Swan points out that in southwestern mythology, "blue clothing [signifies] women with a state of power." She adds that "women of power favor blue silk clothing and shawls."[17] Father Olguin notices that Angela "placed a blue scarf about her head, opened the gate, and walked through the yard to the chapel" (HMD 29). Angela is surrounded by the color "blue," yet her own indigenous color, "white," is also emphasized throughout. "White" is the Pueblo/Navajo color of the east, the "white of the fourth world below this one where . . . coyote is the sacred animal."[18]

Similar to *Coyote* who is on the one hand "a member of the Holy People's community, companion, helper,"[19] and on the other hand the mischievous trickster figure in southwestern mythology, Angela wavers back and forth between being vengeful and helpful. *Coyote*'s amoral and self-serving aspects reveal themselves all too clearly in Angela. When Abel answers her inquiry for someone to split firewood and then refuses to bargain for his wage, she is put off, feeling that it "remained for her to bring about a vengeance" (HMD 33). Also, she "would have liked to throw him off balance, to startle and appall him, to make an obscene gesture, perhaps, or to say, 'How would you like a white woman'?" (HMD 35). When he passes in front of her on the Feast of Santiago, "she was ready again to deceive. She smiled at him and looked away" (HMD 43). On the other hand, as we find out much later, she was one of the few people who offered him her friendship and tried to help him find a job outside the reservation.

Not only the way Angela looks but also her thoughts place her firmly within the framework of Native American mythology. During her first encounter with Abel, Angela displays a remarkable sensitivity towards and a knowledge about him. With great perceptivity she observes how he "leaned into the swing" and how "the blade flashed and struck" leaving "the wood gaped open" like a wound hard to heal. She senses that Abel spends "some useless agony . . . upon the wood, some hurt she could not have imagined until now" (HMD 33). In accord with her mythological counterpart, *First Woman*, who initially faced the problem of finding an appropriate identity, Angela "wondered who she was" (HMD 34). Instead of an answer, she starts thinking of bears, the sacred animals of the west.

> She would have liked to touch the soft muzzle of a bear, the thin black lips, the great flat head. She would have liked to cup her hand to the wet black snout, to hold for a moment the hot blowing of the bear's life (HMD 34).

Angela also blends into the directional symbolism of southwestern mythology. Whereas in her whiteness she had personified qualities of the east, Angela is now, as the day draws to a close, increasingly surrounded by yellow, the color of the north, the color that conveys the Pueblo "notion of personhood."[20] In "the soft yellow light," while picking up the wood Abel had chopped, she senses "the sacramental violence which had touched the wood" (HMD 36). She once again becomes aware of Abel's utter pain when in the evening she watches "the yellow-white flames curl around the wood, seeming never to lay hold of the hard, vital core" (HMD 37). Able to see beyond the war veteran, the man lost between the outside world and reservation life, Angela immediately recognizes Abel's mythic dimension. When she first wonders about Abel's personality she compares him to the Cochiti Corn Dancers she had watched earlier:

> Angela thought of . . . the way he looked at her. . . . A few days before she had seen the corn dance at Cochiti. . . . There was something so grave and mysterious in it, those old men chanting in the sun, and the dancers so . . . terribly serious in what they were doing. No one of them ever smiled. Somehow that seemed important to her just now (HMD 37).

It is hardly surprising that Angela feels drawn to the Corn Dance since she, in her role as *First Woman*, symbolizes the transformation of corn into human form. Her description of both Abel and the dancers foreshadows the "runners after evil" Abel notices years later. They too are described as serious, passing "in the night, full of tranquility, certitude" (HMD 96). It is this image of men running for power and strength that will promote Abel's change towards health and balance, as it is his participation in the race that will conclude his process of integration.

Angela observes the Feast of Santiago which takes place within "four corners," with a "fresh hole in the ground, about eight inches in diameter . . ." (HMD 41, 42). The days of origin return in this setup which clearly represents the sacred four corners of the Pueblo and Navajo worlds with "shipap," the Place-of-Emergence, in the middle. Angela perceives the drums "echoing on and on in a region out of time" (HMD 42), the sound losing itself in "time immemorial," the place where dreams and ceremonies occur, the place where all sacred stories take place.

During the chicken pull, part of the Feast of Santiago (the patron saint of the Pueblo), Abel appears out of uniform for the first time. His efforts to reenter the life of the community through participation in this event, however, are compromised by an albino who, after skillfully plucking the buried animal, pins Abel against a wall and beats him with the bloody rooster. The albino rides through the Pueblo on a black horse, a "perfect commotion, full of symmetry and sound." Yet Angela is not fooled by her momentary fascination. With all of her senses keened she senses the albino's eventual destiny, noticing "something out of place, some flaw in proportion or design, some unnatural thing" (HMD 43).

The ceremony is effecting Angela in fundamental ways. On a physical level she feels a "strange exhaustion of her whole being" (HMD 45); on a metaphysical level she is capable of shedding all the negativity that had at times surrounded her. Her mind and thoughts are encapsuled in the ceremony, and her body is left "to recover without her . . ." (HMD 45). Through the ceremony, Angela has acquired a keen sense of her environment, an understanding of the interrelatedness of all beings. Thus, the ceremony has fulfilled its purpose: the emotional and psychological integration of the individual into the larger community of mankind. What has been denied to Abel, Angela has achieved through her participation: she has left behind the isolated, individual personality and is now restored to conscious harmony with the universe. The ceremony has provided her with the opportunity to "become literally one with the universe," to lose "consciousness of mere individuality and share the consciousness that characterizes most orders of being."[21] Angela even identifies with the sacrificed animal, remembering that, at the "same sacrificial hour of the day," she had "lain with a man. . . . for a long time on the edge of sleep, empty of the least desire, in the warm current of her blood" (HMD 45).

The Feast of Santiago marks a turning-point in Angela's life. For the first time she has an inkling of the meaning of ritualistic events and the significance they hold for tribal existence. She recognizes both the practical and social aspects as well as the purpose of ritual-organized activity to direct nonmaterial energies toward some larger goal. She is beginning not only to understand, but feel within herself, that the ceremonials restore the psychic unity and unbroken continuity of the people, reaffirm the terms of their existence in the universe, and validate their sense of reality. She finally comprehends that the ceremonials form the foundation of tribal culture.

Whatever message exists in ceremonial acts, according to Gill, "is not nearly as important as its power to evoke a network of images related to sense experiences, moods, emotions, and values."

> This evocational aspect is borne not only in the form of rhythmic repetition and the language of the words but also, and perhaps to an even greater extent, in the context and texture of the ritual act of prayer - the sounds, sights, smells, stories, songs, ritual gestures, and dance movements that inform the experience.[22]

Consequently, when Angela returns home that night she is "alive to the black silent world of the canyon." Now she is not only enveloped by "black," the color representing the fourth sector of the sky, the night, but actually uses that color to "create." In accordance with her newly found metaphysical sense of reality, Angela turns into a creator figure, "creating the wind at her window out of the cold black stillness that lay against the walls of the canyon." The objects and forces of nature are no longer static, but now possess a life-force. Angela gets further intuned with the world of southwestern mythology where animals represent powerful spirits when *Mountain Lion*, the sacred animal and 'spirit of the North,' appears before her, holding her in its "queer, momentary gaze [and] burning on in her vision for a time afterward, brighter than an animal's eyes, brighter at last than the windows of the Benevides house . . ."

(HMD 52-53).[23] Having reached that reality where "thought and feeling are one, where objective and subjective are one,"[24] even Angela's house has acquired a purpose. Secret "like herself," it is "no longer the chance place of her visitation," but "the dominion of her next day and the day after." For Angela, the Benevides house now assumes a timeless dimension; it turns into an "organic mass the night had heaved up, even as long ago the canyon itself had been wrenched out of time . . ." (HMD 53). Like people in ritual-based cultures, Angela now perceives the universe--and even man-made objects--as alive, aware, and organic.

For Abel, on the other hand, the ritual was yet another proof that "his return to the town had been a failure" (HMD 56-57), that he is still a stranger to his people, unable to relate to their traditions and beliefs. Whereas Angela perceives a creative power within herself and views her environment as a related organism, Abel feels displaced like the "bits of drift that bobbed and hung among the stones." Unaware of his part in the mythic context he hurries towards Angela's home, the "high white walls of the Benevides house" (HMD 58). The concept of "home" is of utmost importance in southwestern mythology for "the power a being controls is brought out by a description of its home. . . ."[25] Since the whiteness of Angela's home is stressed repeatedly, it might well be associated with the Night Chant's "House of Horizontal White,"[26] White-House in Canyon de Chelley, mythical home to both Navajos and Keres:

> The upper story of White House . . . is painted white; the lower story is the natural yellow of yellow sandstone. The Navahoes do not think this the result of a mere whim, but that it is intentional and symbolic. White is the color of [the] east in Navaho symbolism, and they suppose the upper story was sacred to . . . Talking God, who was a god of dawn and of the east. Yellow is the symbolic color of the west, and they suppose the lower story belonged to . . . House God, who was a god of the west and of the evening twilight.[27]

In this context, Angela's close proximity to her Navajo prototype is established through *First Woman*'s habit of occasionally wearing "masks something like the masks worn by *Haashch'éeltí'í* the Talking God . . ." (Diné 52). *Talking God*, co-creator of *First Woman*, spiritual grandfather to *Monster-Slayer*, and one of the prime spirits related to White House, is also the leader of the Night Chant, the ceremony which aids in Abel's eventual healing process. It is within these sacred walls, the home of his mythological "grandfather," that Abel's transformation and eventual physical and psychological recovery begins.

Whereas Abel seems to have acquired a western sense of time and hurries towards his work, Angela, having left the Los Angeles world of 'time is money', has now entered an environment where time is of no concern. She waits for Abel "for days, without caring how many" (HMD 58). When she hears him approach she decides to take a bath. The bath is a symbol of paramount significance in Navajo mythology since it encourages the change from the profane to the sacred and "transforms a person from evil or neutral to holy." The bath which "originated in the fourth world to change the then existing creatures into godlike forms,"[28] helps prepare Angela for her mythic responsibilities. After her purification, when "the last line of light had risen to the rim of the canyon wall" (HMD 59), Abel and Angela make love. Throughout their love-making Angela is aware of the mythic dimension intruding upon her consciousness. The sacred dimension of the episode becomes apparent in the color and animal imagery used. Blue, the sacred color of the west, and *Bear* and *Badger*, the sacred animals of the West and the South respectively, appear repeatedly in Angela's mind. Surrounded by "soft blue light" (HMD 61), Abel, for the first time since his return to the Pueblo, knows exactly "what he was doing." Reminiscent of the stature of a bear, his mythical prototype, he "was dark and massive above her, poised and tinged with pale blue light." The mythic dimension is not lost on Angela who thinks of "the badger at the water," and perceives Abel as "the great bear, blue-black and blowing" (HMD 62). This specific combination of colors, the "black-blue pair," Reichard writes, "is found in the Mountain Chant,"[29] in which both *Badger* and *Bear* figure prominently. Years later, Angela will narrate a story reminiscent of the Mountain Chant, thereby providing Abel with a mythic role and helping him achieve health and wholeness again.

Bear and *Badger*, as directional animals, also function as the prime spirits of medicine. *Badger* derives added significance from his role in both Pueblo and Navajo origin myths, thereby linking the love-making scene to the primordial beginning of creation. While most animals came to life only after the people emerged through the fourfold underworld onto the surface of the earth, *Badger* not only participated in the emergence but even aided the spirits living underground in the process. Two females had been born and lived underground at a place called Shipapu. According to *Ts'its'tsi'nako's* (*Thought Woman*'s) orders they had planted a tree to push a hole through the earth. Soon they noticed that the hole the tree had made was not big enough for them to pass through, "so Tsichtinako [sic] advised them to look again in their baskets where they would find the image of an animal called dyu'p (badger) and tell it to become alive."

> They told it to live, and it did as they spoke, exclaiming, "A'uha! Why have you given me life?" They told it not to be afraid nor to worry about coming to life. "We have brought you to life because you are to be useful." Tsichtinako spoke to them again, instructing them to tell Badger to climb the pine tree, to bore a hole large enough for them to crawl up cautioning him not to go out into the light, but to return, when the hole was finished. Badger climbed the tree and after he had dug a hole large enough, returned saying that he had done his work. They thanked him and said, "As a reward you will come up with us to the light and thereafter you will live happily. .

You will always know how to dig and your home will be in the ground where you will be neither too hot nor too cold."[30]

Angela's increasing connectedness to her environment is further emphasized in the description of her body as "supple and round" (HMD 61), which nearly matches the subsequent description of the rocks and soils as "supple and soft" (HMD 62). Absorbed in her environment, she seems to merge with nature, listening

> to the sound of thunder and of rain that fell upon the mountain miles away, that split open the sky and set an awful tremor on the trees. She heard the touch of rain upon the cones of evergreen spines, heard even the laden boughs bending and the panes of water that rose and ran upon the black slopes. . . . She had a craving for the rain (HMD 68).

The rain, like the bath earlier, engenders a change towards holiness. The land responds to Angela's desire, and "the clear aftervision of the rain, which she could still hear and feel so perfectly as to conceive of nothing else, obliterated all the mean and myriad fears that had laid hold of her in the past" (HMD 71). Since rain and storm are considered allies that "not even monsters can survive" (Dine 261), the supernaturals are certainly on Abel's side when he kills the "alien presence" (HMD 63). The rain Angela desires so profoundly is the same rain that Abel feels when he murders the albino. The man is not portrayed as an individual but as a malicious force within the Pueblo social structure, as a symbol of the ancient evil in human nature. At the moment of his death, the albino embraced Abel and "drew him in close, and the terrible strength of his hands was brought to bear only in proportion as Abel resisted them" (HMD 78):

> He seemed to look not at Abel but beyond, off into the darkness and the rain, the black infinity of sound and silence. Then he closed his

hands upon Abel and drew him close. Abel heard the strange excitement of the white man's breath, and the quick, uneven blowing at his ear, and felt the blue shivering lips upon him, felt even the scales of the lips and the hot slippery point of the tongue, writhing. He was sick with terror and revulsion, and he tried to fling himself away, but the white man held him close. The white immensity of flesh lay over him and smothered him. He withdrew the knife and thrust again, lower, deep into the groin (HMD 77-78).

Like in his love-making with Angela and during the Dawn Race at the end, Abel knows exactly how to proceed without having to think. The killing of the albino is not, as Schubnell maintains, "an attempt to annihilate his own confused self,"[31] but instead a true and necessary ritual:

And Abel was no longer terrified, but strangely cautious and intent, full of wonder and regard. He could not think; there was nothing left inside him but a cold, instinctive will to wonder and regard. He approached and knelt down in the rain to watch death come upon the white man's face. He removed the little black glasses from the white man's face and laid them aside, carefully (HMD 78).

The ritual nature of the crime becomes further apparent during the trial. In the courtroom Abel is surprised at the judges' attempt to explain the crime in terms of the western legal system. With great astonishment Abel hears the judges debate his motives for the murder. None of their reasons come even close to the truth:

He had killed the white man. It was not a complicated thing, after all; it was very simple. It was the most natural thing in the world. . . . They must know that he would kill the white man again, if he had the chance, that there could be no hesitation whatsoever. For he would know what the white man was, and he would kill him if he could. A man kills such an enemy if he can (HMD 95).

The rain that Angela had so intently prayed for, the rain that had washed away the drought, also washes away Abel's crime. Just as the rain left the fields "bright and clean," it falls on the knife making it "clean" (HMD 80, 78). The forces of nature, unleashed by the ceremony and additionally called forth by Angela, are in support of Abel's "crime."

The murder takes place in the white man's world, near a highway and a telephone pole. However, Abel does not follow the moral codes of a "white" environment, but instead abides by the age-old truths of his tribal upbringing. Stirling mentions that in ancient times it was sometimes necessary to kill a human enemy in order to get accepted into the respected Warrior's Society; more often, as in Francisco's case, the capturing of an eagle or the killing of a bear was sufficient.[32] In modern times it is in accord with Pueblo belief to "ceremonially" annihilate evil. Pueblo ritualism offers, what Ortiz calls, "mock violent" accounts of both the scalp and the war ceremonies in which the "threat of violence is real enough. . . ."[33] Whereas the killing of the eagle, making its strength unavailable to the people, is considered a crime according to tribal ritual procedure, the annihilation of the albino, the evil aspect of the Pueblo world, is a crime only according to the western legal system. "Murder," Wyman points out, "is potentially dangerous not because of the deed itself but because of contact with the dead."[34] Although Abel understands the presence of evil, he does not yet know how to deal with it in a tribally sanctioned manner.

Part II, "The Priest of the Sun," an allusion to the Kiowa Sun Dance, opens six years later with an image of grunion cast upon a California beach. Like Abel, they are vulnerable and out of their element. The story then shifts immediately to the Los Angeles church of John (Big Bluff) Tosamah, an urban Native American peyote priest.[35] He is the focus of a community of relocated tribal people, including both Abel and his Navajo friend, Ben Benally. The first part of the second chapter consists mainly of Tosamah's homily on St. John's gospel, "In the beginning was the Word . . ." (HMD 85-91). On the following pages Tosamah reveals the similarities that used to exist between Christian and Native American beliefs. Once, he claims, there was only this one sentence in Christianity, "'In the beginning was the Word' [and] *that* was the Truth, the bone and blood and muscle of the Truth." And right then and there St. John "should have stopped." But he could not

> let the Truth alone. He couldn't see that he had come to the end of the Truth, and he went on. He tried to make it bigger and better than it was, but instead he only demeaned and encumbered it. He imposed his idea of God on the everlasting Truth (HMD 87).

By demonstrating that one of the main theistic concepts of Native America, the sacredness of the word which "came from nothing into sound and meaning" (HMD 89), once also existed in Christianity, Momaday creates a common basis for both belief systems. Both creation myths, Native American as well as Christian, once held the eternal, the sacred truth. Since wholeness for the protagonist in <u>House Made of Dawn</u> is obtainable only through reaching back to the original myths of his tribe, the same--Momaday might imply here--is true for Christians as well. Westerners do not have to adopt Native American ways; they have their own "native" roots. But the white man is "sated and insensitive [in] his regard for language" in contrast to Native Americans who "are as children [to whom] the Word is sacred . . ." (HMD 89-90). Since children, according to Tosamah, have a more direct and spontaneous connection to the intuitive element of religion, Native Americans have easier "access" to their past and the healing powers connected to it. The way back to the 'Truth', back to the roots of one's origin, might therefore be more difficult, although by no means hopeless, for Christian civilization as well.

The second part consists of Abel's memories as he lies on a cliff near the ocean, following a second beating by the cop Martinez. He remembers the grunion, the peyote services, and his trial, where Fr. Olguin had argued that Abel had killed what he thought was a witch (HMD 94). The thought of the grunion "filled him with sad, unnameable longing and wonder." Abel further realizes that he "could not understand the sea," that "it was not of his world." Instead, "it was an enchanted thing . . . for it lay under the spell of the moon. It bent to the moon, and the moon made a bright, shimmering course upon it . . ." (HMD 91). Although the moon still seems distant and strange, his "recognition of the moon's universal power to order and control the universe reflects Abel's growing reattunement"[36] to the beliefs of his people. In the Southwest the moon, together with the sun, functions as the measure of the yearly cycle in the life of the community. It is of prime importance in both hunting and weather control. As opposed to the sun which is recognized as male, the moon is significant in its connectedness to female power and influence. The sun, as pointed out before, played an important part in Abel's ceremonial upbringing. Yet, in all of the Keresan myths which bear close resemblance to the Navajo creation story, "the moon is important [since] Kochinako, or Yellow Woman . . . is the Moon-Mother of the War Twins, the Sun being their father."[37] The *War Twins* are the Pueblo version of the Navajo heroes, *Monster-Slayer* and *Born-of-Water*. Having lost his natural mother in "reality," Abel lost his *Moon* mother in his function as *Monster-Slayer*. It is of prime importance that Abel now starts to connect to the moon image again, thereby allowing his mother, his female energy, back into his life. Abel, hurt by a childhood devoid of any positive female images, now realizes the existence of his mythological family. Attaching himself to his mythic mother, he now allows *Moon* to awaken pre-childhood memories.

As with the ocean the moonlight forms a bridge in Abel's mind, slowly bringing back memories of his formerly undiluted belief in traditional values. Suddenly he remembers an injured bird in the moonlight and its "bright black eyes, in which no terror was" in the sight of death (HMD 110). Abel now recalls that aspect of his tribal tradition that considers dying part of the natural cycle of existence and death. In his study of religion, God is Red, Vine Deloria, Jr. points out the wisdom of the traditional Native American belief concerning death. What recommends tribal religions, says Deloria, is their perception of a necessary harmony between man and nature and their acceptance of death as part of a natural and cyclical order. "Immortality is secondary to integrity of tribal existence in the present, and we find not a cringing fear of death but a religious community so strong as to virtually shrug off death as an enemy."[38] Abel's loss of identification with his heritage had led him away from a natural view of death and contributed to the immense fears which are haunting him now. At this turning point where memories begin to piece together, Abel realizes the gap that exists between himself and the tribal values instilled in him. As a result of his inability to define himself in a tribal manner, his life is out of balance:

> Now, here, the world was open at his back. He had lost his place. He had been long ago at the center, had known where he was, had lost his way, had wandered to the end of the earth, was even now reeling on the edge of the void. And the sea reached and leaned, licked after him and withdrew, falling off forever in the abyss" (HMD 96).

Abel's reflections attest to his growing reattachment to native values; yet, unlike his friend Benally who talks of Beautyway and the Path of Pollen, Abel is still incapable of articulating a song or prayer to help him integrate his divided psyche. At the moment of greatest despair, when he is sure that his body, like his mind, "had turned on him [and that] it was his enemy" (HMD 93), he remembers his love-making with Angela: "Angela put her white hands to his body. Abel put his hands to her white body" (HMD 94). By focusing completely on her "whiteness," Abel once again evokes the power of the moon which, "according to Reichard, "is white."[39] Abel's "rediscovery of his native heritage appears to be a result of his reattunement to a lunar rhythm."[40]

and he begins to allow the power of the moon, the female energy, back into his life. Like the grunion who are connected to the lunar cycle and who are led by instinct as to the "rightness" of their action, Abel slowly rediscovers the intuitional knowledge of right and wrong. In this state of transformation, under a "moon-bright sky" (HMD 95), Abel perceives an animal of tremendous import in the context of the Night Chant, the owl. The typical prayer to *Owl*, "My feet restore for me, my legs restore for me," ensures physical endurance for the participant of the Night Chant.[41] Guided by his *Moon* mother and attended by *Owl*, Abel remembers the mythic past and envisions the near future:

> There was a faint vibration under him. *Be quiet!* He had to be quiet; something was going on. [He] . . . hurried on in his mind, holding the owl away in the corner of his eye. The owl watched him without meaning, and something was going on. There was the faintest tremor at his feet. The night was infinite and serene, and there was an owl in the darkness and a tremor in the earth. He got down on his knees and put his ear to the ground. Men were running toward him. He left the road and hid away in the brush, and soon he could see them in the distance, the old men running after evil. . . . They ran with great dignity and calm, not in hope of anything, but hopelessly; neither in fear nor hatred nor despair of evil, but simply in recognition and with respect. Evil was (HMD 95-96).

Abel is in accordance with the Pueblo and Navajo world view when he realizes that evil is part of the wholeness necessary to keep the world in balance. Although his visions are still blurred, Abel finally has a faint knowledge of his part in the mythic context. By realizing the interrelatedness of all elements in the universe, Abel discovers that he, too, has a legitimate place in it. Like the protagonist in Part II of the Night Chant who "seeks to identify his mind and body with the minds and bodies of gods [and] strives to project himself into the realm of mythic time,"[42] Abel attempts to find his authenticity in the characters of "time immemorial." And while Abel still hides from the "runners-after-evil" at this point, their imagined appearance nevertheless forecasts his eventual participation in the age-old ceremony and thus his reentry into the world of tribal ritual.

Part III, "The Night Chanter," narrated by Abel's friend Benally after Abel had left to return home, focuses on the problems of Abel's adjustments to the city and the inability of the Relocation Program to compensate for his emotional and spiritual losses. Roommates in Los Angeles, Benally and Abel share many things in their backgrounds. On his one visit to Walatowa, Benally finds the landscape in the Pueblo similar to the Navajo reservation where he grew up. He even suggests that he is somehow related to Abel since the Navajos have a clan called Jemez. Moreover, Abel's father may have been a Navajo, and Abel's grandfather, Francisco, regards the Navajo children who come to Walatowa during the Feast of Santiago, as "a harvest, in some intractable sense the regeneration of his own bone and blood" (HMD 72). In Ben, Abel finds both the brother he had lost many years ago as well as his mythological twin, *Born-of-Water.*

Abel has trouble keeping a job or manage his relationships with Benally and Milly, the social worker. Instead, he drinks more and more and expresses himself only through outbursts of rage. The "only way you can live in a place like this," Tosamah states, "is to forget about the way it was, how you grew up and all" (HMD 135). Neither Abel nor Ben, however, are able to deny their tribal upbringing. To keep Abel going, Benally shares with him a dream of getting back together on the reservation:

> He was going home, and he was going to be all right again. And someday I was going home, too, and we were going to meet someplace out there on the reservation and . . . we were going to get drunk for the last time, and we were going to sing the old songs. We were going to sing about the way it used to be, how there was

> nothing all around but the hills and the sunrise and the clouds (HMD 133).

Benally is the "Night Chanter," his roommate, friend, and colleague who helps introduce Abel to the traditional poems and songs. The "House Made of Dawn" prayer is sung in the Night Chant as part of the Purification section of the ceremony. It is accompanied by a rite in which a set of eight prayer offerings is used to bless or purify the patient. A patient participating in a Night Chant offers himself on the last morning of his healing to the rising sun, breathing in the breath of dawn. Although Abel refuses to speak about the old ways, he still shows an interest in Benally's words:

> 'House made of dawn.' I used to tell him about those old ways, the stories and the sings, Beautyway and Night Chant. I sang some of those things, and I told him what they meant, what I thought they were about. We would get drunk, both of us, and then he would want me to sing like that (HMD 133).

As Gill notices, the message of chants and prayers is highly redundant due to dense repetition. "The verbal elaboration of the prayers and the related ritual elements," he maintains, "is greatly out of proportion to the extent of the semantic messages of the prayers." Yet, Gill is aware that there is more involved in chants and prayers than the semantical referential meaning in the text. "We must ask," he insists, "to what extent and in what ways prayer is more than a conveyance of encoded messages." In order to uncover the most significant aspect of Navajo ceremonial acts, he introduces the term "performative utterances." Similar to Momaday who insists on the immediacy of religious experience through language, Gill describes performative utterances as a group of words the saying--and to a similar extent the hearing of which--equals the doing of an action.[43]

The songs from both Beautyway and Night Chant are designed to attract good and repel evil. They comprise the restorative and exorcising expressions of the very balance and design in the universe Abel perceived in the "runners after evil." The semantic structure of the various prayers is identical with the effect it seeks, that is, the restoration of health, harmony, and balance. Benally's words from the Night Chant are particularly appropriate for Abel, since the purpose of this chant is to cure patients of emotional imbalance:

> House made of dawn,
> House made of evening light,
> House made of dark cloud,
> House made of male rain,
> House made of dark mist,
> House made of female rain,
> House made of pollen,
> House made of grasshoppers . . . (HMD 134).

Dawn is balanced by evening light, dark cloud and male rain by dark mist and female rain. All things are in **balance** and **control**, the two most important features of Navajo and Pueblo religion.[44] By repeatedly hearing the Night Chant and thus participating in the performative function of language, Abel reestablishes a formal union with his tribal heritage. "Restore my voice for me. Restore my feet for me." The race at the end shows that both on a psychological as well as on a physical level his requests have been granted.

Through Benally's mentioning of tribal values Abel gets reacquainted with his tribal tradition. Slowly he approaches his spiritual heritage. By telling Milly to leave the spider alone that had been trying to make a web across his suitcase and by calling it his "roommate" (HMD 162), Abel, even if only on a superficial level, attaches himself to his people's awe and respect for *Grandmother Spider*.

When Abel accidentally sees Angela St. John in Los Angeles, Benally remembers that he "kept saying that . . . she liked him and was going to help him some way" (HMD 161). At first, Benally is skeptical but finally he realizes that Abel is telling the truth:

> When he got hurt . . . he talked about her and said her name, and he was hurt bad and out of his mind, and you could tell that he wasn't making it up. It's funny, but even at first, when I thought he was kidding around, he acted somehow like he knew all about her and she was special and good and she liked him a lot (HMD 161).

When Abel is in the hospital, Benally calls Angela who comes to see him. What seems to be a polite visit to a sick acquaintance turns out to be a meeting that forever alters the course of Abel's life. With her story of the bear and the maiden, Angela relates a message necessary to create the very balance Abel has been yearning for. Benally describes the scene:

> She went on talking kind of fast, like she knew just what she wanted to say . . . and she started telling him about her son, Peter. . . . Peter always asked her about the Indians, she said, and she used to tell him a story about a young Indian brave. He was born of a bear and a maiden . . . and he was noble and wise. He had many adventures, and he became a great leader and saved his people. It was the story Peter liked best of all, and she always thought of *him*, Abel, when she told it (HMD 169-170).

Angela St. John finally gives meaning to St. John's gospel, "In principio erat Verbum," that Abel had heard at the "Holiness Pan-Indian Rescue Mission" upon his arrival in Los Angeles:

> There was only the sound, little and soft. It was almost nothing in itself, the smallest seed of sound - but it took hold of the darkness

> and there was light; it took hold of the stillness and there was motion forever; it took hold of the silence and there was sound. It was almost nothing in itself, a single sound, a word - a word broken off at the darkest center of the night and let go in the awful void, forever and forever. And it was almost nothing in itself. It scarcely was; but it *was*, and everything began (HMD 85).

The word stands for what it signifies. It has both the power of destruction and the power of creation. At his trial, the judges were "disposing . . . of him in language, *their* language" (HMD 95); now, language, *his* language, becomes the tool of his restoration. The way everything in creation began with the word, Abel's whole being gets restructured and reunited in Angela's story. With the narration of a mythic story, the conscious and the unconscious mind are "united through the magic of symbolic progression so that the symbols can . . . stir indirect memories and insights that have not been raised to conscious articulation." This, Allen adds, "heals [and] makes us whole."[45] By identifying Abel with the child born to a bear and a maiden who became the savior of his people, Angela provides Abel with a myth to live by:

> A bear! A bear and a maiden. And she was a white woman and she thought it up . . . made it up out of her own mind, and it was like that old grandfather talking to me . . . and he was going on with his work and talking, going on about all he knew, and he knew everything and there was no end to the stories and the songs (HMD 170).

Angela's story stirs up memories of the adventures of *Older Sister* (*Bear Maiden*) from the Navajo Mountain Chant. The myth of Mountain Chant, or Mountainway, along with that of Beautyway, branches off from the origin legend of Enemyway which relates the Navajo raid on Taos Pueblo.[46] The myth of Mountainway is told to cure illnesses caused by witchcraft and sorcery. The main characters in both Beauty- and Mountainway are two sisters whom *Monster-Slayer*, leader of the attack, had promised as prizes to the warriors who could secure scalps from two "non-sunlight-struck" (virgin) Pueblo girls. Two undesirable elders succeed in obtaining the scalps. Their legitimate claims are ignored and a series of competitions is set up in the hope of younger men beating them. Although the two old men are consistently victorious in all events, the girls are withheld from them. Once the war party returns home, a war dance is held to celebrate their victorious attack. During this celebration the two women follow the sweet smell of tobacco, just to find two handsome young men sitting around a campfire. Upon awakening the following morning, they realize their mistake, for their partners are not only revealed as the same old men they had encountered during the attack, but as *Bear Man* and *Big Snake Man* in disguise. While fleeing from their unwanted suitors *Older Sister*, trying to hide in the mountains, learns Mountainway from the *Holy People*, while the younger sister who escapes to the Plains acquires Beautyway. Both women return with their particular chantway or healing ceremony to give to the people.

The Mountain Chant incorporates two major motifs: "Raised by Bear" and "Protagonist Feigns Death." According to most accounts, *Older Sister* bears a male child which she leaves during an attack on her home by bears. The female bear, feeling sorry for the child, decides to raise it as her own. Eventually however, a famine strikes which leaves the bear no choice but to kill the boy in order to survive. Warned by *Wind*, the boy runs away. Four times the bear catches up with him, but the boy is always able to escape again. Finally, the bear lets him go, telling him where to find his people. The boy eventually marries the older daughter of a medicine man, having himself become powerful and influential. At one point, he feigns death in order to seduce his wife's younger sister. When she finds out who he really is she abandons their child. The boy is subsequently found and raised by an owl.

In "The Night Chanter," the two major motifs are reversed. Leland C. Wyman who has recorded "Mountainway" in all its variations, notes only one instance in which an informant reverses the two major motifs of the myth. Sam Akheah from Rock Point, Arizona, told his version of the myth to Aileen O'Bryan in late November 1928. He reversed the two major motifs and thus, "Raised by Owl" precedes "Protagonist Feigns Death," making *Owl Boy* the protagonist of the subsequent event. Wyman remarks that Akheah's version, coming as it does at the end of the story,

> rather left the myth hanging without a logical sequel, and probably sensing this, he remarked about the offspring of the owl boy and his sister-in-law which was abandoned by his mother, "This baby was found by the Bear." He did not, however, go on to relate *Raised by Bear*.[47]

The last sentence of the myth related in House Made of Dawn, "The child was found by the Bear" (HMD 171), is clearly reminiscent of Akheah's version. The boy who is then raised by the bear is the grandson of *Older Sister*, the originator of the Mountain Chant. The way *Bear Man*, the boy's grandfather, committed a sin by seducing *Older Sister*, Abel's grandfather, himself a successful bear hunter, committed a sin by first sleeping with the daughter of the witch, and then abandoning her with the dead child. *Older Sister* leaves her child out to die, Porcingula's child is still-born. The similarities do not end here. Abel's father--who would be *Owl Boy*--is unknown; like *Owl Boy's* family, nobody in Abel's family remembers--or wants to remember--where he came from or where he went. Continuing this line of thought, Abel would be the "child found by the Bear."

Angela's story inspires memories of the Mountain Chant in Benally and succeeds in creating a different past and a more hopeful future for Abel. Instead of suffering from both his grandfather's unacceptable act and from his own status as a fatherless, possibly illegitimate, child, Abel is now furnished with a new mythic background. At the same time Angela's story prepares the way for a future no longer devoid of tribal recognition and integration. The image of the bear Angela had perceived at the beginning of their acquaintance has come full circle: during their love-making Abel relives and **corrects** his grandfather's past behavior as *Bear Man*; then, while lying in utter desperation on the beach he meets his father, *Owl Man*: "So far had his vision reached that the owl . . . seemed to fly in his face and break apart, torrential, ghostly, silent as a dream" (HMD 95). By reliving the past of his ancestors, Abel removes the spell. He has appeased the supernaturals and won *Bear* as a mythic companion on his way towards tribal integration. From now on the supernaturals will be on his side.

Although Benally had taken Abel through a step-by-step process of visualization before, singing parts of the Night Chant ceremony, Abel has only partly been capable of understanding the power words hold and the sacred action they contain. With her story, however, Angela fills that void, taking up the thread left by Tosamah's grandmother a long time ago:

> When [grandmother] told me those old stories, something strange and good and powerful was going on. [She] was taking hold of my imagination, giving me to share in the great fortune of her wonder and delight. She was asking me to go with her to the confrontation of something that was sacred and eternal (HMD 88).

Speaking and thinking are a form of action. Reichard comments: "The Navajo believe, in common with many Native Americans, that thought is the same or has the same potentiality as word. To thought and words they add deed, so that there is no use trying to differentiate."[48] Words are actions that have the ability to align and heal. This concept is the basis for the Night Chant in which the patient identifies with the gods, goes on a symbolic journey, and is made holy. By the patient's visualization of the action, the action itself occurs and the patient is restored. "The healing that takes place beyond language," according to Allen, "comes of the resonance, the after-image of speech in the imagination." The visual energy remains, having been sparked by words.

Restoration follows language, and as energy, "language contains the potential to restore us to a unity with earth and the rest of the universe."[49] Momaday writes in The Man Made of Words:

> We are what we imagine. Our very existence consists in our imagination of ourselves. Our best destiny is to imagine, at least, completely, who and what, and *that* we are. The greatest tragedy that can befall us is to go unimagined.[50]

Regarded in light of Momaday's philosophical approach, Angela's story bears great powers. What is named will appear. Abel will become the "Indian brave," noble and wise who will eventually save his people. He will once again display aspects of *Monster-Slayer*, prototypical hero of the Navajo creation myth. With her story Angela reawakens the mythological hero in Abel; at the same time she turns herself into the quintessential story-teller of southwestern legends. In the great tradition of *Thought Woman*, the Pueblo creatrix whose every idea turns into reality, Angela continues the cycle of creation by handing Abel a vision to live by. Like the Navajo's *Spider Woman* who provides *Monster-Slayer* and *Born-of-Water* with a formula "that would quiet the anger of enemies,"[51] Angela hands Abel a story designed to help him overcome both his emotional as well as his physical "enemies." Abel's ability to see, to imagine himself at the end of the novel, is the result of language, more specifically, the language Angela St. John uses, the language of the creation stories. The way *Monster-Slayer* overcomes his enemies, Abel finally possesses the tools to overcome the monsters within and is now ready to accept his newly won identity. Like *Monster-Slayer*, whose "failures are attributed to ignorance, not to evil intention," and who, although originally human, becomes holy "through trial, error, and divine dispensation," Abel achieves "wholeness."[52] His odyssey, his vision quest, has ended.

Part IV, "The Dawn Runner," shows Abel attending to his dying grandfather. Abel "had been there six days at dawn" (HMD 175), and "the old man had spoken six times . . ." (HMD 177). The Pueblo/Navajo holy number "six," signifying the four directions as well as zenith and nadir, foreshadows Abel's integration into the mythic framework of his ancestors. Francisco had been mumbling words that make no sense to Abel. On this last night, however, he recounts memories that further Abel's healing process, touching upon his relationship with the land, whites, and his community. Francisco's memories climax in his successful bear hunt and in the race he had run as a young man. Both he performed perfectly. Although "he had begun at the wrong pace, another and better man's pace," that moment "passed, and the next and the next, and he was running still . . ." (HMD 187-188).

Before dawn Francisco dies, and Abel ceremonially prepares his grandfather's body for burial. His ritual response to his grandfather's death helps him rise above the fear and uncertainty he had experienced before. He wakes Fr. Olguin, demands that he bury Francisco, and turns away abruptly. Then, after first stopping to cover his body with ashes from an oven near the edge of the village, he joins the Dawn Runners racing for rain and fertility in the new year. Blackened with ashes Abel runs the Race of Dawn, the race towards the east. Black, in combination with the eastern direction, "represents protection from danger"[53] in mythological narratives. In addition, the mountains are covered with rain, "an indication that supernatural events [are] taking place."[54] As the dawn rain begins to fall, washing the ashes from his body, he recalls Benally's "House Made of Dawn" prayer from the Night Chant: "There was no sound, and he had no voice; he had only the words of a song. And he went running on the rise of the song" (HMD 191). Once the voice is restored the patient is "capable of freer, less constrained expression." Zolbrod adds that "restoration of the highest human faculty in its proper turn equals full recovery - removal of the 'spell'" (Dinė 13).

Because House Made of Dawn is structured after ritual patterns, the novel's resolution lies in Abel's willing and knowledgeable participation in the ritual pattern that inform his tribal life. That is, he not only needs to engage in ritual practice but also understand his proper role in the scheme of things. Abel sets out to parallel his grandfather's deeds, like *Monster-Slayer*, his mythical prototype, and *Born-of-Water*, had done when they had run against their maternal grandfather, *Talking God*:

> Once more, the boys started quickly. And they immediately set a pace they never relinquished. For the entire distance of the race they neither heard the voices of the two gods nor saw them, so fully did they outrun them. . . . When *Haashch'eelti'i* the Talking God and *To neinili* the Rain God finally crossed the finish line they were pleased and had this to say: "Well done . . . grandsons. . . . You have grown into what we wanted you to become. Perhaps now you can well serve those who have nurtured you (Dinė 177-178).

Abel runs the Dawn Race, a symbol of fortitude and strength, qualities that please the gods. The race becomes a tie with his ancestral and cultural past and helps him achieve full psychic and physical integration. At the end of the novel, Abel "could see at last without having to think." And beyond his pain Abel sings silently, "House made of pollen, house made of dawn. Qtsedaba" (HMD 191). Since Abel successfully completes the race as his grandfather had done before him, he will grow into what Francisco had wanted him to become: both a man fully integrated into tribal life as well as a successful bear hunter. Thus he will fulfill Angela St. John's prophecy. As *Haashch'eelti'i* assures *Monster-Slayer* in the last two lines of the Night Chant:

> Thus will it be beautiful,
> Thus walk in beauty, my grandchild.[55]

iii.

N. Scott Momaday

Grey and Changing Woman

The Ancient Child Reborn

> The book I'm writing now is itself a legend, not only a kind of investigation of the legend-making process, but is itself the legend-making process.[1]

Momaday's latest novel, The Ancient Child, is framed by a foreword, a prologue and an epilogue. Paying tribute to the Pueblo/Navajo holy number "four," The Ancient Child, like House Made of Dawn, is divided into four "books." Similar to the construction and ultimate completion of a painting, the four segments progress from "Planes" over "Lines," to "Shapes" and "Shadows." These segments are then again divided into non-sequential, numbered parts. At times, these parts are preceded by a poem and/or mythological excerpts. Just as in House Made of Dawn, the novel's mythic significance is established repeatedly. In addition to historical flashbacks, the novel contains numerous Kiowa and Navajo mythical elements. The first part of the novel, for instance, starts out with "Ah-keah-de: *They were camping*" (AC 14), which Momaday writes in The Names, is the traditional beginning of a mythological tale.[2]

The novel tells the story of Grey, a young Kiowa/Navajo woman whose visionary power enables Set, a famous painter of Native American heritage, to experience his ultimate destiny in life. At first glance Set seems to be a person who has everything anybody could want in life. Beneath the surface layer of fame and fortune, however, there is a person deeply dissatisfied with his own existence. Through Grey's medicine power Set recognizes the significance his people's myths hold. By reliving the myth pertaining to his individual destiny he is eventually able to fulfill his human potential.

Interspersed in this contemporary tale is the "Wild West myth" of Billy the Kid and his various exploits and escapes.[3] At a younger age, Grey had read The Saga of Billy the Kid which had affected her so deeply that "she swooned and ran a temperature of 103 degrees" (AC 17). Ever since that time she had imagined herself in the role of Billy's lover. At first it is through visions and dream sequences that Grey overcomes the chronological gap of almost a century, thereby becoming a participant in Billy's adventures. What first seems like a futuristic trip into the past, however, eventually turns out to be a combination of different layers of time. The figure of Billy the Kid, the mythic hero of the 'Wild West', takes Grey "too far in the fantasy," that is, "beyond that point at which she wanted the dream to end" (AC 226). To the degree that Grey's teenage "affair" with the Western hero/outlaw thus approaches its historically set, violent end, her mature, psychic connectedness with Set grows. By taking actions that Grey cannot control anymore, Billy leaves the realm of her imagination and takes on a life of his own. On a literary, historical, and mythic level, the interaction between vision and reality, time-bound and timeless experience, narrative melting of past and present, is thus complete.

The first book, "Planes," begins with the well-known Kiowa story of *Set-talee, Bear-Boy*, which forms the prologue and is repeated throughout the novel. The legend tells of eight children, seven sisters and their brother who play until suddenly "the boy was struck dumb" and "began to run upon his hands and feet." His fingers "became claws, and his body was covered with fur."

> Directly there was a bear where the boy had been. The sisters were terrified; they ran, and the bear after them. They came to the stump of a great tree, and the tree spoke to them. It bade them climb upon it, and as they did so it began to rise into the air. The bear came to kill them, but they were beyond its reach. It reared against the trunk and scored the bark all around with its claws. The seven sisters were

> borne into the sky, and they became the stars of the Big Dipper (Prologue).[4]

The story takes place at Tsoai, or "Rock-Tree" (officially called the "Devil's Tower National Monument" near Sundance, Wyoming). The laccolith--called Tso'-saw,"Rock Shelter" by the Kiowa and Mato-tipi, "Bear-lodge" by Black Elk's people--stands 5,117 feet above sea level and served for centuries as a landmark for the northern tribes. The place-name yields Momaday's first Native American name, Tsoai-talee, or Rock-Tree Boy. In House Made of Dawn, Tosamah, Momaday's alter ego, describes the rock:

> There are things in nature which engender an awful quiet in the heart of man; Devils Tower is one of them. Man must account for it. He must never fail to explain such a thing to himself, or else he is estranged forever from the universe (HMD 120).

Besides the prologue, the first chapter includes an excerpt from an "Ethnographic Dictionary of the Navajo Language," and twenty-four numbered parts which differ in length. The portion from the dictionary introduces the Navajo word for "bear" and his various parts, as well as the requirements necessary to conduct the Mountain Chant.

As has been mentioned in the House Made of Dawn section, the Mountain Chant (Mountainway) recounts *Bear Man*'s pursuit of *Older Sister*. When she finally reaches the home of the Holy People they teach her the Mountain Chant, instructing her to relate the legend to all Earth Surface People. In House Made of Dawn, the myth of Mountainway serves primarily as a stimulant supposed to trigger symbols of "time immemorial" and memories of a seemingly long forgotten heritage. In The Ancient Child, on the other hand, not the effects of a retelling of the myth, but its content and purpose are explored. The Mountain Chant is designed specifically to cure people afflicted by "bear" disease. "Bear disease," writes Wyman, "seems to be firmly associated with two groups of illnesses, arthritis and mental disturbances."[5] He further notes, however, that "Navajo curing ceremonials are directed toward appeasing or exorcising the etiological factors supposed to have caused the patient's troubles rather than toward the physical symptoms of the illness itself."[6] The etiological factors Mountainway deals with are connected to animals which inhabit the mountains, first and foremost the bear.

Bear sickness may be contracted through a great variety of injuries or insults to this animal. Set never had any physical contact with a real bear; however, his last name, "Setman," the anglicized version of his original Native American name, still echoes the name of his animal prototype, the bear. Set, like Set-angya, Sitting Bear, famous chief of a Kiowa soldiers' organization, the Kaitsenko ("Real Dogs") Society, is named after the bear. However, by disregarding the implications of his name, Bear Man, he lost contact to his original ancestry; he adopted a "white" name and "white" ways to the complete exclusion of his native heritage. Everybody calls him "Set" or, even worse, "Loki," the evil god of Germanic legend, "Unheilschmied . . . Verleumder und Betrüger der Götter. . . ."[7] By choosing to disregard the significance of his real name, Set avoids his real purpose and destiny in life. Names in Native American thought are more than words--they are a destiny, a vision of the future, an homage to powerful mythic spirits whose magical powers they contain. A path has been laid out for Set, a story has been told about him. He will have to walk down that path and he will have to relive that story. As Momaday writes in The Names, "a man's life proceeds from his name, in the way that a river proceeds from its source."[8] In The Man Made of Words, Momaday responds to the question: "What is an American Indian?" as follows:

> The answer of course is that an Indian is an idea which a given man has of himself. And it is a moral idea, for it accounts for the way in which he reacts to other men and to the world in general. And that idea, in order to be realized completely, has to be expressed.[9]

People belong and act according to the names they bear, the language they are born into and grow through, and the stories they are known by. By not using his real name, by not expressing his Native American roots, Set's "idea of himself" is necessarily different from the destiny embodied in his heritage. Until Set learns to have the proper "idea of himself," his reaction to people and the world is irreconcilable with his real purpose in life. This dichotomy between the concept Set has of himself and the concept bestowed upon him by his heritage leads to the eventual disintegration of his emotional being. Early on in his life there were signs that unmistakably demonstrated both the danger and the prophecy embodied in his name. One day as a child in the foster home he was stung by "bee-wolves," which according to Sister Stella Francesca, is "an old, old name for bears." The "anger of the holy ones," maintains Haile, is certain when an arrow or a similar object is "lodged in the patient's interior."[10] When afterwards the "sting resulted in an extraordinary swelling" (AC 74), his participation in a mythical context is guaranteed since throughout the myths, "there are constant references to the hero's or heroine's sore, aching, swollen limbs."[11] As has been mentioned prior, there are a number of parallels in Kiowa culture highly suggestive of southwestern ceremonies, including the swelling up of joints as a sanction against trespass, the holy number four, the purification ritual after return from supernatural encounter or adventure, the bundled fetish, and the use of a bear claw necklace as medicine. Also, "killing a bear produces sickness, unless exorcising ceremonial is performed [sic]."[12] Set will need to participate in a healing ceremony in which an "exorciser" symbolically removes the weapon or dart. This ceremony, called the "shock-rite," is a necessary ritual to render the patient impassible to similar attacks.

In the first chapter two of Set's closest friends are introduced, Lola Bourne, his girlfriend, and Bent, his adoptive father. When he receives a telegram from Oklahoma telling him that his paternal grandmother is dying, Set decides to go more out of curiosity than of sorrow. On this trip he meets hitherto unknown relatives, among others Grey, the self-proclaimed "Mayor of Bote, Oklahoma" (AC 67):

> Her father was Kiowa and her mother Navajo, and the two cultures came together in her easily. . . . English was the language of her childhood home at Lukachukai, but she hoarded bits of the Kiowa and the Navajo languages as she could (AC 17).

Angela St. John in House Made of Dawn had to first overcome the obstacles of her cultural background before realizing her mythic potential and help Abel to realize his. Grey, on the other hand, already combines the prerequisites of a woman in touch with her mythic counterpart. She is the controlled, balanced counterpart to Angela's willful and impetuous character, just as *Changing Woman*, the only "consistently virtuous supernatural in the Navajo world"[13] is the advanced archetype to *First Woman*'s fragmentary and rudimentary features:

> Changing Woman . . . is the most fascinating of many appealing characters conjured up by the Navaho imagination. . . . She is the mystery of reproduction, of life springing from nothing, of the last hope of the world, a riddle perpetually solved and perennially springing up anew. . . .[14]

Like *Changing Woman* whose first appearance was rather mystical,[15] Grey also, "just turned up one day," she "just appeared, came from nowhere, it seemed." And Kope'mah, the wise old medicine woman, "liked her most of all, and she didn't seem at all surprised to see her [like] she was expecting her" (AC 67-68). Similar to the Navajo goddess, who "grew remarkably fast, developing with miraculous speed,"[16] Grey, although barely nineteen, "can talk like an old, old woman" (AC 69). Furthermore, *Changing Woman's* love for horses whose creator she is finds its equivalent in Grey's attitude towards her mare:

> Even led at a walk, its energy and strength were near the surface, so that it seemed about to prance or wheel or rear up. And in the same moment she determined to have it, not to own it in the ordinary sense but to have it at the disposition of her will, to the extent that the creature would allow it, to have it in her hands and between her legs, to count it among the things that defined her (AC 27-28).

In Grey are connected a wild, untamed spirit as well as a deep, psychic understanding of the ways of the medicine woman Kope'mah, her great-grandmother. Grey had spent the last months at Kope'mah's side, realizing that she is the one chosen to take on her medicine power. As opposed to Angela's initially rather indistinct vision, Grey, like *Changing Woman*, has a clear vision of her destiny. She is endowed with supernatural power which does not depend upon instruction:

> Grey had not to struggle with the words, for she was not listening at the level of language but beneath it, in the deep recesses of the imagination. And then they were two women, the storyteller and her listener, telling and told the ancient emergence of light. . . . Kope'mah seemed a child, drawn into Grey's embrace, her little bones angled into the young woman's supple bust (AC 34).

The merging of Kope'mah and Grey, the simultaneity of old and young, the "timeless rejoicing [that] entered into their veins, into the current of their common blood" (AC 34-35), is reminiscent of *Changing Woman*'s ability to transform herself from an old woman to a young girl. As she stands in the house of *Sun*, her sons, *Monster-Slayer* and *Born-of-Water*, are startled by her appearance:

> They saw a medium-sized woman who took a White Shell Cane in her hand and went east and returned much younger than before. She went south and her hair was gray when she came back. She went

> west and came back old and white-haired, and when she went north she went slowly and stopped. After this she looked at them awhile, and then she went east again, coming back as a beautiful maiden.[17]

Changing Woman's cosmic cyclic movements--aging with winter and becoming a beautiful young maiden each spring--make her the essence of death and rebirth, responsible for the continual restoration and rejuvenation of life. Similarly, Grey's acceptance of Kope'mah's healing powers guarantees the ongoing rebirth of the medicine woman's visions which the tribe depends upon for continuance.

Shortly before her death, Kope'mah startles Grey by her remark that "'The bear is coming'." That night, in an episode reminiscent of both Angela's bear phantasy while making love to Abel and the Kiowa tale of "Star Girl" (as mentioned under endnote # 4) in which a young woman every day meets her lover, "a bear who licked her and hugged her,"[18] Grey dreamed of sleeping with a bear who "drew her into its massive arms and licked her body and her hair" (AC 29). Like Angela, Grey has a vision of the future. Yet, whereas Angela was unaware of the prophetic relevance of her initial visions, Grey is confident enough in her growing abilities as a medicine woman to realize the mythic potential of those revelations.

Miles away, Set who "had made a considerable reputation, having received several important awards and attracted the attention of critics and collectors throughout the country" (AC 36), finally realizes that "he had squandered much of his time and talent," and "had become sick and tired" (AC 38). Set paints, as he himself admits, to "relieve the terrible boredom of God."

> Surely we humans, even with our mother-in-law, ceased to amuse Him many ages ago. What sustains Him is the satisfaction, far deeper than we can know, of having created a few incomparables - landscapes, waters, birds, and beasts. He takes particular pride in the

> stars, and it pleases Him to breathe havoc upon the oceans. He sighs to the music of the desert at dawn. The eagle and the whale give Him still to ponder and admire. And so must He grieve for the mastodon and the archaeopteryx. And the bear -- ah! He used both hands when he made the bear. Imagine a bear proceeding from the hands of God! (AC 39)

Like Abel in House Made of Dawn, Set has "no mother or close maternal relatives and, therefore, no home in the Navaho sense. . . ."[19] He also lost his mother at a young age; only dreams of her, which often turn into a philosophic discourse, are left. Unlike Abel, who realized only after traumatic suffering the significance of a balanced universe, Set is aware of the necessity of opposites:

> And he dreams of his mother's touch [and] the dream becomes a story, a myth. Ritual has a place, so have good and evil, and there is an ineffable intimacy. Nothing is unnatural, and there is no question of right and wrong. There is merely a moment in the rite of passage, the irresistible accumulation of experience (AC 43-44).

Thinking that "they had nothing to do with him, [that] they were his relatives, but . . . not his family" (AC 51), Set nevertheless decides to visit his dying grandmother. When he arrives in Oklahoma, a strange and hitherto unknown feeling comes over him, "as if some ancestral intelligence had been awakened in him for the first time . . ." (AC 64). He is aware that he could not "even begin to see the design, but perhaps he would see it clearly in time" (AC 63). For the first time he experiences "not genesis in the public domain . . . but *his* genesis" (AC 64). Seeing Grey from afar, he initially mistakes her for a boy: "The boy looked at me, looked inside me, through me, even" (AC 67). This ability to change and assume many shapes further attests to Grey's identity with *Changing Woman.* Set's feelings towards her are less than favorable in the beginning: "He didn't know what to make of things. Who the devil *was* this Grey, anyway, and what right had she to intrude upon him?" Still, he realizes that her presence "was strange and evasive [and] that it inhabited another world . . ." (AC 102). He feels powerless, like he "had been moved about like a checker on a board. He had been made to appear, pulled out of a hat by a magician, a trickster, a sorceress . . ." (AC 104).

When Set hears that Kope'mah had talked about him in her last days, he feels he "narrowly missed an opportunity to know something about himself, something of who he was" (AC 71). Shortly before returning to San Francisco, Set experiences his first contacts with Native American ceremonies. He attends a dance where he meets Grey again who wears "a buckskin dress . . . and buckskin boots" (AC 111).

> Mythologically buckskin is an emblem of life; ritualistically it is a life symbol: Creation, really transformation, was accomplished by laying corn, precious stones, or both between buckskins. Restoration is brought about in much the same way - the properties and procedure are almost identical for transformation from inanimate to animate and for restoration from unconsciousness or death to life.[20]

Grey embodies all the qualities Set needs so desperately. She, like *Changing Woman*, is the emblem of life and rejuvenation, she is the recurrence of spring after winter and life after death. Set, on the other hand, a man of immense fame and fortune, is deeply dissatisfied with life. He paints for people and money and perceives himself a traitor to the arts. Whereas Grey symbolizes the certainty of physical and spiritual transformation, Set embodies the materialism and emotional instability which characterized his ancestors in the lower worlds. Like Abel, Set too starts to disintegrate physically and at one point is incapable of speaking. Only "animal-like . . . groans and growls" (AC 73) emerge from his lips:

> To speak seemed the most important and necessary thing in his life, to rise from some profound and primitive helplessness to the level of speech; but he was prevented by some monstrous resistance in himself, it seemed. And the most terrible thing was, he did not even know what he wanted to say, *had* to say, if only he could say it (AC 73-74).

At the dance ceremony Grey asks Set to paint her face. Since according to Kiowa custom "a man would paint his wife's face . . . in token of his affection,"[21] Set, without realizing it, enters into a relationship with Grey far beyond the limits he can presently imagine. Grey chooses the colors blue, yellow, black, and red, which correspond to the colors of the four lower worlds and symbolize the emergence to the Fifth World. Instructed by her grandmother, Grey also gives him back the bundle containing the bear-medicine, "his" medicine:[22]

> Grey held it out to him. He took hold of it, but she did not give it up at once. For a moment in which he thought they must have been engaged in ritual, they held the bundle between them. . . . Ordinarily, he would have been extremely uncomfortable at such a moment, but in fact he was altogether at ease and at the same time strangely stimulated. . . . There was a burning at his eyes, and he had a vision of the grandmother, little and shriveled in her coffin, strangely like a child. And he . . . felt he had laid his hands to death, that he had come into the presence of the darkest power - until this moment he would have named it "evil" - he had ever known. And he was exhilarated beyond belief (AC 115).

The events of creation are in many ways paradigmatic for Navajo lifeways. As exemplified in this passage of The Ancient Child, the possession of a mountain-soil bundle--inseparably connected to the creation of *Changing Woman*--has not lost any of its significance in Navajo culture since the days of creation. *Changing Woman* showed the Navajos how to make a bundle modeled on hers; this was the origin of the mountain-soil bundle. It is made with soil ritually collected from the four sacred mountains which mark the borders of the Navajo world. The soil from each mountain is wrapped in buckskin. With the bundle and the Blessingway songs and prayers, which commemorate her existence, *Changing Woman* represents the power of creation, and as such, she is the source and sustenance of all life, and the mother of the Navajo people.

Looked at from the perspective of mythology, Grey's gift to Set has far reaching implications. In her function as *Changing Woman*, Grey possesses the power of creation and transformation contained in the bundle. By handing the bundle to Set she hands him those powers. She therefore provides him with the ability to transform himself, to create himself anew. The medicine bundle, both "a source and a repository of sacred power"[23] obviously contains paramount forces; after receiving it, Set starts to have frightening dreams and senses an intrusion that he can neither identify nor resist. "Something seemed to be taking possession of me. It was a subtle and pernicious thing; I wasn't myself" (AC 145).

Even after Kope'mah's death, the old woman's spirit still speaks to and through Grey, teaching her the old ways and foreshadowing the new. Through dreams Grey and Kope'mah enter into a supernatural communication. Since "no one except the jish [medicine bundle] owner has the right to decide to whom the jish should be given,"[24] Grey visits her grandmother's grave again and again to be sure:

> Does he have a vision and a song? Can he suffer and delight hugely, anciently, with respect and belief? And is he then the bear, Grandmother?

And Kope'mah's answer is unmistakable: "Yes. Yes. Yes. Yes" (AC 116).

Their "healing materials and methods, their 'magic' or paranormal competencies," Allen writes, come to the visionaries "through dreams or vision-based concourse with the world of the spirit people, the Grandmothers. . . ."[25] Persistently, Grey becomes "more confident of her learning, of her power, of who she was and of what her purpose was" (AC 228). The bundle containing the bear medicine which holds such frightening power for Set, has a very different meaning in Grey's frame of reference. She "had passed to Locke Setman the bear medicine. In that initial moment had been power and mystery and meaning; the proprieties had been observed, the giveaway had been accomplished, a marriage had been made" (AC 174). Moreover, Grey is deeply aware of the meaning of this ritual: "Locke Setman . . . was the name of the man who would require her strength and wisdom and spirit . . ." (AC 174).

Like Abel in Los Angeles, Set is filled with strange and disturbing visions and struggles with the power that is increasingly taking hold of him. Through his frightening dreams and memories which seem to surface more persistently, he notices that his transformation had started a long time before he encountered Grey. Talking about the picture of "a grotesque man with red hair and red dress" which he had begun "with nothing but color in mind [and which] had taken form quickly and of itself," Lola Bourne had remarked that "the little man [is] about to be transformed" (AC 106, 107). "Red," according to Reichard, is the "color of danger, war, and sorcery. . . ."[26] It is also the color of the First World from which pre-human creatures struggled to the upper worlds seeking an exit. The people in the lower worlds instinctively felt that they needed a place larger and brighter to inhabit. The dwarf he created is the unconscious embodiment of Set himself, trapped, like his ancient mythical forebears, within the confining walls of a limited consciousness.

Set starts to remember a story his father, Cate, had told him many years ago. It is the tale of a young boy who wanders into a Piegan camp one night and, without knowing either the language or any of the people, feels at home right away. Though they are suspicious at first, the people nevertheless let him spend the night. The next morning the little boy is gone. The people are worried and the delicate balance of everyday life seems disturbed. The most shocking thing about the boy is that he did not give his name. "As far as the Piegans were concerned, the little boy had no name. And do you see, Loki," Cate continues, "this matter of having no name is perhaps the center of the story. Words are names" (AC 121). An old medicine man understands the importance of names and finally finds a way to account for the mysterious event: he tells his tribe that the boy never existed; instead, it was a bear who had lost his way and had trailed through the camp. People are relieved and able to go on with their daily lives. But from that time on "their story must forever contain the story of the boy" (AC 120), the boy who through their tales and eventually their legends, turned into a bear.

The story emphasizes the importance and the power of language to create or undo existence. The boy did not exist because he did not have a name. The story also forecasts Set's psychological transformation into his mythological prototype, the bear. Like the boy who wandered into the camp and the boy who became a bear at Tsoai, Set has to turn "bear" and "legend" in order to play his part in the myths of his ancestry. Only by consciously acting out his "story" within and through the ancient rituals will he appease the supernaturals and introduce meaning and balance to his existence. His survival, like Abel's recovery, lies in his people's rituals and in his conscious participation in them. Not until he relives part of his mythic heritage will Set achieve his true destiny and restore sanity to his disenfranchised mind. Momaday sums up the essence of the first chapter: "An ancient woman inhabits the body of a girl. . . . The bear comes forth. Planes" (AC 123).

The legend of *Bear-Boy* and "the little sisters to whom it happened" (AC 129), also introduces "Lines," which comprises a poem plus twelve parts. In the second chapter, the third-person narrator is at times abandoned in favor of the more personal "I" narrator, thereby emphasizing Set's increasing emotional instability. Set returns to San Francisco and although feeling physically and emotionally drained, initially continues on his path of painting and exhibiting. He starts talking to himself, realizing that on his trip to Cradle Creek, "something happened [and] what happened was something that began a long time before that" (AC 136).

As of now he cannot define his emotions, yet he senses that they all "point to a time and place in the past, maybe the remote past." He feels that he is "trying to bring some crucial memory, deeply buried, to the surface . . ." (AC 140). His state of mind finds expression in his paintings:

> There were many of the dark figures in my work now. I didn't know how to account for them. They were a kind of fascination to me. They seemed endlessly vital and mysterious. And they *were* self-portraits in a sense, for they expressed a certain reality in me. I didn't know what it was, but I knew *that* it was, and I knew that it mattered greatly to me in some way. And it was coming closer and closer to the surface of my thoughts; I was going to recognize and understand it sooner or later, and that act of understanding or recognition was going to be of the deepest importance to me (AC 144).

Slowly, Set becomes emotionally unstable, "unhinged, neurotic, obsessive" (AC 138), and experiences bouts of schizophrenia and occasional seizures. "There was no longer a design to his existence. His life was coming apart, disintegrating. . . . His whole being suffered a numbness, a kind of paralysis" (AC 215). It is again a woman who forecasts Set's eventual transformation: Alain Sancerre, an art gallery owner from France, sees in his painting "Venture Beyond Time," a centaur, a man who had become one with an animal. Set's creative impulse is connecting him to his roots, the Kiowa, who became "centaurs in their spirit" at one point in their history. Alain connects her observation with Kafka's description of centaurs, called "Wunsch, Indianer zu Werden [sic]" (AC 161). Her comments foreshadow both Set's own merging with an animal as well as the centaur-like man who performs the "shock-rite" ceremony on Set, enabling him to reach back to his heritage.

On the way back from an exhibition, Set becomes dizzy and starts to tremble, exhibiting all the common physical manifestations of fear. He starts having frightening dreams of being a child again, "moving inexorably toward a black point, the very center of the darkness" (AC 140). Set is drawn to the very beginning of his existence, to the Place-of-Emergence which "is depicted in black because it represents the origin of all things."[27] The more Set disintegrates, the more the powers initiated and unleashed by Kope'mah and Grey become effective. That mythical powers watch over him becomes apparent when the color "red" which had surrounded the dwarf, his "lower" self, now gives way to a "red-black combination." According to the Navajo color symbolism, this combination functions as a safeguard against danger and sorcery. While in a playful mood, Lola Bourne creates a "shield," painting "serpentine stripes, red and black, on [his] chest and back and on [his] arms" (AC 157). Like *Monster-Slayer* who was protected from the initial wrath of *Sun* by a "blanket of red dawn [and a] black shroud of darkness" (Dinė 206), Set, protected by an armor-like color scheme, is able to embark upon his journey. He remembers the medicine bundle that he had stored away without ever seeing its content:

> I had been afraid of it. I had told no one about it. I had pretended that it did not exist. But now it seemed to pervade my mind. I had a nearly overwhelming desire to be with it, to be wholly in its presence, close to it, to lay my hands upon it (AC 158).

To the same degree that Set disintegrates, Grey becomes steadily more conscious of her spiritual and psychic abilities. Instructed by both her grandmother and "the earth, eagles, fishes, coyotes, tortoises, mice, and spiders," she gains a profound insight into "remote distances of time and space." Just as Set has to follow his destiny, Grey needs to fulfill her predetermined course. Unlike him, however, she has long been aware of her purpose in life: "She had not decided to be a medicine woman. . . . She was becoming a medicine woman because it was in her to do so; it was her purpose, her reason for being; she *dreamed* it" (AC 173). Dreams constitute an important way of entering into a supernatural dialogue, a way of establishing a relationship with the Holy People.

The Dreamer "is the mother of the people," says Allen, "because she gives them life through her power of dreaming. . . ." The Dreamer is "the center of psychic/spiritual unity of the people," and the "life force that is passed to the Dreamer from the nonmaterial planes is embodied in . . . ritual objects, and garments. . . ."[28] Grey is becoming a mediary between the world of spirits and the world of humans. Every night she goes into Kope'mah's room, to "put on the grandmother's moccasins and aprons and shawls" and to touch "the walking stick, the comb, the beaded pouch that had belonged to the grandmother" (AC 176). Kope'mah's belongings connect her to the beings and events of the lower worlds, to the voices of "animals and birds and insects, of leaves rustling and water running, of the endless wind" (AC 202). Both Abel in House Made of Dawn and Grey in The Ancient Child receive the gift of tribal values from one of their grandparents; while Abel listens to his grandfather involuntarily, however, Grey consciously tries to emulate her grandmother's ways.

The end of the second chapter also marks the end of Grey's preoccupation with Billy the Kid. Billy had taught her that to be a legend is to be immortal. To be immortal means to participate in the lives of people forever. His story strengthened her belief in the immortality of legends. However, to the extent that her responsibilities towards her mythic part in an ancient ritual grow, her obsession with the legend of her adolescence subsides into the background. By writing a journal, "The Strange and True Story of My Life with Billy the Kid," Grey turns herself into a part of his *story*, not his life, thereby leaving her imagined historical persona in favor of her present-day existence. The oral tradition celebrates the contemporary viability of stories. But since Grey now chooses to limit her "life" with Billy to the printed page, she actively confines that part of her life to the past. Dreams of Lukachukai, the Navajo village of her upbringing, now fill her whole being.

Although apart from each other, both Set and Grey share the conviction that there is only "one story" and only one preeminent concern: they "*must be true to the story*" (AC 217). They must follow the ancient, prescribed rituals. Although there is no physical connection between the two, Grey knows exactly that he will return and that he will return soon:

> It was something, his coming, that she could bring about - had indeed already brought about - by the sheer strength of her will and her belief. Her will had been expressed in dream and in ceremony. It could not now be brought into question, much less aborted (AC 248).

Grey's ability to control the future secures her place in the pantheon of supernaturals. Whereas Angela, at the outset of her encounter with Native American spirituality, considered employing strategies and trickery to achieve the desired goal, Grey is naturally endowed with psychic powers. Here the difference between the potential of divinity, as exemplified in the basic structure of *First Woman*, and the certainty of divine knowledge, as *Changing Woman* possesses it, becomes manifest.

Only when Set's emotional and physical disintegration reaches an unbearable degree does he return to Oklahoma. He turns himself over to Grey, realizing that "she would be his mentor. She would instruct him." As opposed to Set, Grey knows of the story about "the ancient child, the boy who turned into a bear" (AC 229, 174), and is fully aware of the task ahead of him. Set has stopped painting; it now becomes obvious that his art formerly functioned as a further estrangement from reality. He will now have to face the essence of his being without the artistic buffer-zone, head on.

The third chapter, "Shapes," which includes a Navajo poem plus five parts, describes their move from Oklahoma to Grey's Navajo hometown of Lukachukai. At times, Set asks himself why he gave up the life of a famous West Coast painter in order to live a rather primitive life in a far off Navajo village. Grey reminds him of the story they will have to complete:

> Don't imagine that you have a choice in the matter, in what is going on, and don't imagine that *I* have one. You are *Set*; you are the bear; you will be the bear, no matter what. You will act accordingly, in the proper way, because there is no other way to act (AC 271).

On their trip Set starts to vomit which according to Navajo belief is part of the purification rite, thus considered an important part of the overall cure. Set is at the very beginning of his metamorphosis: "A low, terrible sound came from his throat, like guttural laughter, like a growl. He was grotesquely poised on his feet, his back hunched, and he was helpless" (AC 278). Set has now demonstrated all the common forms associated with bear disease: nervousness, fainting, temporary loss of mind, and a violent irrationality. Grey knows that the Mountain Chant is the preferred treatment of such manifestations of bear disease. She is well-qualified to aid in Set's healing process: besides being a visionary and a medicine woman, Grey is, like the original twelve people involved in the Pueblo Raid (which marks the beginning of the Mountain Chant), a descendant of the Bitter Water Clan. Even their journey to Lukachukai marks a return to the beginning of the Mountain Chant tales since the "Lukachukai Mountains . . . figure prominently in the locales of the stories."[29]

On their way to Lukachukai Grey asks Perfecto Atole, a Jicarilla Apache medicine man and "keeper of a bear's paw" (AC 284), to perform the "shock-rite," a bear ritual. "In times past," writes Wyman, "the ritual hunting of bears was practiced in order to obtain their paws to make medicine bags for the Mountain Chant [and] their claws to attach to pouches made from buffalo or buckskin in the shape of a bear's paw. . . ." The shock-rite, Wyman maintains, "is employed when the patient has been subjected to direct attack by the etiological factors involved - struck by lightning, bitten by a snake, mauled by a bear."[30]

> The offender has not so much injured or abused the animal form, as he has the human or supernatural form of the animal in question. Because of his actions or omissions, therefore, this supernatural being, not his animal garment, is 'exercising a hold' on the transgressor. In native conception this supernatural always reminds the transgressor through sickness or indisposition of some kind.[31]

In Navajo ritual an impersonator of the animal or god frightens the patient during the "shock-rite." This exorcistic ritual "aids the patient in his struggle to free himself of the supernatural . . . injury."[32] Henceforth, "the latter is not only immune to all danger from the deity impersonated, but may even count upon him for protection." Ever since the time that *Changing Woman* had told accompany the newly created Navajo race on their travels towards a new homeland, Bear has been commonly held in high esteem for his protective power.[33] After having experienced the shock-rite and having been "reborn," Set will also be able to count on *Bear*'s protection.

The scene of Set's bear ritual in which a man with a bear paw on his right hand frightens and strikes him (AC 286), is reminiscent of the sandpainting "Bear's Den" which commemorates the "shock rite." In the sandpainting, the "personator of the bear, the north black figure, will enter as a bear and frighten the patient. . . ."[34] The total identification of the bear and the patient is achieved since the bear is actually considered a symbol of the patient himself. Like the patient in the sandpainting ritual, Set is absolutely terrified:

> He was weak and disoriented. He had no breath, no strength. . . . His eyes and lungs were burning, and there was no feeling in his legs. Then the hoofbeats and the loud, rushing rattle of the shakers came suddenly upon him, SHUH, SHUH, SHUH! and he pivoted to his right, to no avail (AC 287).

After Set is struck in the throat with a bear's paw by the centaur-like medicine man, he, like the patient in a successfully completed sandpainting ritual, feels that "something of his will's power was unaccountably restored to him" (AC 288). Since "the colors of the sun: red and yellow and orange and gold" (AC 284), are illuminating the morning sky, it becomes apparent that Set is under the protection of *Changing Woman*'s divine "husband." According to Reichard, *Sun*'s red rising in the east signifies protection and the successful completion of a ritual.[35] Set is finally able to make a morning prayer. This "prayer to Sun" is especially significant since *Bear*, along with *Snake*, *Big Thunder*, and *Wind*, is the guardian of *Sun*'s house. Without *Bear*'s approval, a morning prayer could thus not have been accomplished.

During major rituals, *Changing Woman* was "ceremonially dressed in whiteshell." In order to pay homage to the legendary character of Billy's exploits, Grey, during her participation in Billy's adventures, had always worn "the long white dress [and] had crumpled and kneaded the dress in order to take the stiffness out of it" (AC 76-77). As a "symbol of divinity, white expresses perfect ceremonial control." White, which in Navajo symbolism "differentiates the naturally sacred from the profane,"[36] plays an important part in Set's "shock-rite" ritual also. What must seem an "inappropriate, white dress" to the mere observer, in combination with a "Pendleton blanket, red and black" (AC 284), actually turns the scene into a holy ritual with red and black added for protection. Grey's white garments, signifying the color of the east, counterbalance the "dark figure [that] was approaching from the west" (AC

285), thereby keeping the balance necessary for a successful ceremony. On a physical level, *Changing Woman* saves the world from evil forces by giving birth to *Monster-Slayer*; on a symbolic level, the mere presence of *Changing Woman*, dressed in her ceremonial colors, exerts the influence necessary for man to "extricate himself from uncontrolled forces."[37] Although Grey stands aside during the "shock-rite," her presence is thus not only of prime importance, but indeed wholly indispensable. Set is aware of her significance: "He understood . . . that she knew far better than he what was about to be" (AC 285). Since *Changing Woman*'s ability to give physical birth is a consequence of the power of giving spiritual birth, it is in keeping with mythological truths when Grey, following Set's "re-creation," becomes pregnant soon thereafter.

Settling down with Grey's mother, her sisters, and niece, Set soon becomes deeply grounded in the Navajo way of life. He learns the purification effects of both sweat-emetic ceremonies as well as physical exertion. Sweat-emetic rites are indispensable when "contemplating exposure to danger," like "contact with the supernatural as layman [or] learner."[38] The environment at Lukachukai creates the stable and supportive background which enables him to emotionally relive his boyhood. He realizes that, "in keeping with the story, he must play out his part as Set-talee, Tsoai-talee, boy bear, rock-tree boy" (AC 291).[39] For the first time he recognizes the source of his problem: "The bear stands against me" (AC 295). Set had been named after the bear, yet he had never lived accordingly. He had never listened to his name, had never been able to listen to it. Therefore, his name had never been a source of inspiration for him. Unaware of the story of his life, he had been unable to live it. Now, however, he is capable of saying, "I am the bear" (AC 295).

While Set gathers emotional and physical strength, Grey creates the very situation that makes his development possible. Aware of her psychic abilities and strengthened by her mythic background, Grey easily adapts to her new role as homemaker. "It is the nature of woman's existence", writes Allen, "to be and to create background." This fact, she continues, "viewed with unhappiness by many feminists, is of ultimate importance in a tribal context. . . ."[40] Grey realizes that any progress on the inner journey Set is about to undertake demands the purification of body, soul, and spirit. Like *Changing Woman* who moved west to make a home for her husband, Grey moves west to establish her home with Set. Like the goddess who "made suds for his bath and laid out his clothes, and . . . brought in ceremonial food,"[41] Grey bathes Set and gives him "water to drink and a kind of gruel, made of crushed corn and goat's milk, pinons and dried fruit, and in the manner of Navajo men a hundred years ago, he wrap[s] his loins in white cloth . . ." (AC 296).

The last and smallest portion of the novel, "Shadows," consists of a Sioux poem plus two parts. It describes Set's successful completion of his quest at Tsoai, the rock-tree. It is during the traditional vision quest, enhanced by fasting and the presence of a bundle (which are both ceremonial necessities), that the spirit world and the natural world interconnect most intensely. Continuing the bear ritual which prescribes as a final reconciliation with the animal prototype the venturing out to a place "near a stone or tree turned or moved by a bear," Set returns to the place where the boy became the bear. "In nearly every Mountainway myth," Wyman says, "there is an account of a visit of the hero or heroine to the home of the bears. . . ."[42] Whereas during the "shock-rite" ritual he encountered his mythic prototype without fearing for his life, Set will now have to complete the second and more threatening part of his task. Before partaking in the symbolic re-emergence indispensable for his complete spiritual rebirth, he has to descend to the depth and darkness of the beginning, of the First World. Like the mythical "Navajo protagonist," Set is now "placed in a predicament of superhuman proportions."[43]

Like his ancestors were in the lowest of the four worlds, Set is completely surrounded by water and darkness. Even Tsoai, the massive rock-tree, "lay just ahead of him like a dark body of water" (AC 310). And when "he entered it, it did indeed seem its own element, unlike the earth around it; the air seemed suddenly thinner, darker, colder." When he starts "climbing away from the river toward the rock tree," he embarks on his symbolic ascent to higher spheres which in Native American belief carries all the significance of the *actual* emergence. He makes a camp "on the east side of the rock" (AC 310-311), the direction guarded by bears in the Mountainway myth.[44] Set knows that he must identify and become one with the bear by commemoration and recapitulation of the ancient scene and by the exact imitation of the mythical event. After four days he notices "the stars of the Big Dipper" and perceives "the image of a great bear, rearing against Tsoai" (AC 312). When, in his vision, he turns from a mere observer into the bear himself, when "he heard things he had never heard before [and when] he had no longer a human voice" (AC 313-314), he has achieved his destiny. 'The achieved identity', Cassirer observes,' is not a theoretically realized one, but, because the process of identification was magically experienced and felt, the final identity is indeed believed within a mythic context'.[45] Running on all four legs, Set is still bound by and connected to the earth. Getting up on his hind legs and rearing against Tsoai, however, he finally discovers the Place-of-Emergence, his entrance to the current, the Fifth World. Being restored to psychological balance through the eternal power of the Mountain Chant, Set verifies Allen's notion that myth "functions as an affirmation of self that transcends the temporal [which] allows us to image a marriage between our conscious and unconscious, fusing the twin dimension of mind and society into a coherent, meaningful whole."[46] *Bear*, once a feared prototype, will from now on be his mythic protector. And, like in the Navajo creation story, *Bear* will be the guardian of *Changing Woman*'s home on earth.

In his two novels, Momaday is clearly preoccupied with the personal well-being of his male protagonists. Both Abel and Set are emotionally out of balance; in Abel's case, the instability engulfs his whole being, clearly visible for anybody: he is a drunk and even commits a murder. Set, on the other hand, has seemingly "made" it in the white man's world and is apparently in control of his life. This well-roundedness, however, turns out to be a surface phenomenon. The moment he gets in touch with his Native American past, he becomes emotionally disturbed and fragmented. This disturbance results, as with Abel, in violence against himself and others. By letting Set, a completely uprooted person, find his way back to his native heritage, Momaday stresses the contemporary attraction of Native American myth. For people like Set, thus probably for whites too, the way towards fundamental native beliefs--even if not necessarily Native American--is a possible alternative to the individualization and fragmentation of contemporary society.

Momaday addresses his protagonists' healing processes as a Navajo medicine man would address the creation of a sandpainting. Just as the Navajo healer works outward from the center, Momaday's concern is the well-being of the individual whose spiritual integrity and balance, it is hoped, will eventually heal society as a whole. In his attentiveness towards the individual Momaday follows the Navajos' understanding of ritual and ceremony that a well-balanced individual is the prerequisite not only for a well-balanced tribal existence, but for the very survival of the tribe itself.

Through the characters of his alienated male protagonists, Momaday addresses the mythic significance of his female characters. Whereas the mythic proportions of the protagonists are easily visible, the women's mythic import can only be detected after careful exploration of female supernaturals in the Navajo/Pueblo pantheon of deities. While Angela displays all the traits commonly attributed to the Navajos' first deity--initial hostility, deception, but ultimately the urge to create--Grey is from the very beginning endowed with all the goddess qualities of the Navajos' supreme deity, *Changing Woman.* The male characters figure more prominently; yet, their mythic-spiritual evolution is possible only through the female characters assisting them. Only with their guidance can Abel and Set overcome their spiritual fragmentation and take their due place in Native American ritual and tribal tradition.

There is, however, a marked difference between House Made of Dawn and The Ancient Child. Whereas Abel's actions and thoughts are incomprehensible to most anybody not entirely familiar with Native American beliefs, Set, except for his heritage a white person, acts in ways easily apprehensible. In his second novel, Momaday moved to a synthesis of Euro- and Native American perspectives. This creates a distance which the added explanation and mystification only enlarges: understanding more initially does not mean understanding more eventually. The mythical embeddedness of plot, character, wording, and structure, the entity called House Made of Dawn, gives way to a back-and-forth, however knowledgeable, between two worlds. Instead of being drawn into a world beyond the immediate understanding, a strange world is presented on a golden platter. Yet, the distance, which (ironically) may reflect Momaday's closer connection to the "white" world, remains.

iv.

Leslie Marmon Silko[1]

Ts'eh and Yellow Woman

Earth Mother's Ceremony

I will tell you something about stories,

...

They aren't just entertainment.

Don't be fooled.

They are all we have, you see,

all we have to fight off

illness and death.

You don't have anything

if you don't have the stories (C 2).

"That's how you know . . . you belong," Silko reasons, "if the stories incorporate you into them. . . . In a sense, you are told who you are, or you know who you are by the stories that are told about you."[2] In Ceremony, Tayo, a young Laguna man, participates in the unfolding of a story that eventually heals both him as well as his society. Like Abel and Set before him, Tayo must willingly and consciously become part of the ceremony.

Silko's novel Ceremony resembles Momaday's House Made of Dawn in that it also focuses on the problems of a World War II veteran. Like Abel, Tayo is poor, unemployed, and without plans for a job in the future; furthermore, both men are very much alone in the world with few, if any, ties to friends or community. Due to an overall emotional instability, both face the same problems of integration into their respective tribe. As with Abel, white doctors are unable to cure Tayo's severe mental problems; only through the efforts of Betonie, a Navajo medicine man, and the assistance of three mysterious woman-figures, Tayo achieves a complete physical and emotional recovery. Analogous to House Made of Dawn and The Ancient Child, the end of the novel foreshadows the protagonist's complete integration into the tribal social and religious structure. Silko's Ceremony, however, does not stop there: in sharp contrast to Momaday's novels, which center mainly on the protagonists' individual regeneration, Tayo's spiritual reintegration is inextricably linked to the overall tribal well-being.

Tayo, a mixed-blood Laguna, has been emotionally injured by the desertion of his mother, the contempt of his aunt who brought him up, and the trauma he experienced as a soldier in World War II. Like Abel, Tayo does not know his father, one of his mother's white one-night-stands. In order to emphasize their heroes' despair, both Momaday and Silko have separated their protagonists from their mothers through death or abandonment. Since in southwestern tradition the loss of the mother equals the loss of the entire cultural heritage, each protagonist suffers from an alienation which far supercedes any mere abandonment by any one person.

While Ceremony, like House Made of Dawn and The Ancient Child, is on the surface a tale about an alienated man, it is even more a tale about the power of women. More apparent than in Momaday's novels, Ceremony is filled with symbols which relate to a mythological woman-figure and "through her to the universal feminine principle of creation. . . ."[3] Tayo is (unknowingly) surrounded by a whole cast of mythical female characters: the Mexican captive who had originally thought up the ceremony, Night Swan who aids in its continuation, and finally Ts'eh who, in her function as the goddess *Yellow Woman*, serves as the paramount force behind the ceremony's successful conclusion. These women, all endowed with supernatural abilities, are working to counterbalance the forces of evil witchery threatening to take over the entire world.

Paralleling Momaday's works, the two narrative types in Ceremony "are the contemporary and the mythic tellings, the timeless and the time-bound narratives."[4] The two are not independent of each other in that the mythic narrative constantly foreshadows and comments on the story itself. Silko overtly juxtaposes the mythic and the contemporary portions of the novel by stating the myth in lyrical form to contrast with the prose that carries forward Tayo's contemporary struggles and realizations:[5]

> The mythic material presented in poetic form paces the reality of the prose, leading us to the climax of the novel, but it also comments on the action of the story and gives order. Only when we see the reality of the novel in terms of the mythic poem, do we see the order of the story. The loss of power and vision, or, as Tayo says, "how the world had come undone," the struggle to return the world to its proper order, the successful conclusion of the crisis, and the identity and harmony created by this successful conclusion of the story are all predicted, ordered, and directed by the myth/poem.[6]

"The Laguna story that I follow," says Silko, "is about the mother creator, and it's uncorrupted by Christianity."[7] Appropriately, the novel begins with an invocation of the Pueblo creatrix *Ts'its'tsi'nako, Thought Woman*, who "named things and as she named them they appeared." Silko gives full authorial credit to *Ts'its'tsi'nako*, who "is sitting in her room thinking of a story now" (C 1). *Ts'its'tsi'nako* represents the mythic prototype of the creative artist in the narrative while Silko herself turns into the traditional Pueblo storyteller. Silko's invocation also names *Ts'its'tsi'nako*'s two daughters (or sisters), *Naotsete* and *Uretsete*. The former plays a crucial part in Keresan mythology as the goddess whose anger at human misbehavior caused her to eventually leave the world and withdraw rain and fertility, bringing drought and misery to the people. Only when Hummingbird, Fly, and a few others embark on a long ceremonial quest to regain her favor does she consent to help the people again.

Before the horrors of World War II cut Tayo's link to his cultural heritage, he had believed in the Pueblo prayers and stories and in the power of ceremonies:

> He had picked flowers along the path, flowers with yellow long petals the color of the sunlight. He shook the pollen from them gently and sprinkled it over the water; he laid the blossoms beside the pool and waited. . . . The things he did seemed right, as he imagined with his heart the rituals the cloud priests performed during a drought (C 94).

Consequently, as Tayo completes his rain ceremony and begins to descend the mountain he sees a "bright green hummingbird" (C 95). In the Navajo creation story, Hummingbird was sent by the spirits in the First World to "report on the size and condition of the earth." Hummingbird was in charge of finding water, and after investigating the upper world he "reported water in every direction."[8] In keeping with the mythic story, the sky fills with "low dark rain clouds" (C 96) two days after Tayo's prayer. The thunder preceding the rain comes from the direction of Mt. Taylor, called Tse'pi'na (Woman Veiled in Clouds) in Laguna. Having prayed the rain in, Tayo must now experience its power personally in what turns out to be his first step in the ceremony. Since the rain prevents Tayo's uncle Josiah from meeting his girlfriend, Night Swan, he sends Tayo to the nearby village of Cubero with a message for her.

Night Swan is a mysterious woman. She initially settled in Cubero because she saw Tse-pi'na and, as she puts it, "liked the view." Even for her lover Josiah it remains a secret "what it was about the mountain that caused her to stop there" (C 87). Only later will it become apparent that Night Swan's choice of residence was not a mere whim, but a necessary step in the development of the ceremony. Night Swan--as the anticipation of Ts'eh (who resides at Tse-pi'na)--surrounds herself with objects and garments of blue, indicative of her state of power. As mentioned in the House Made of Dawn section, southwestern mythology attributes great mythic power to the color "blue"; as an important feature in color symbolism it will figure prominently in the discussion of mythical female characters in Ceremony as well. Night Swan wears "open-toe blue satin slippers" and a kimono made of "blue satin." Inviting him in she points "to a blue armchair" in a room painted with "blue flowers." They make love on "blue sheets that were stretched tightly across the bed" (C 98). The color symbolism, Lincoln writes, leads "toward the mountain spirit-woman herself, Ts'eh Montano. Ts'eh gathers blue-flowering herbs in a blue shawl to bring rain to the desert, making medicine the old way, aligning 'blue-gray mountain sage with the blue stone'" (C 184).[9]

As has been mentioned prior, one essential trait of women endowed with mythical power is their closeness to the objects and forces of nature. Natural phenomena are perceived as possessing a life force, a term which roughly corresponds to the western concept of "soul." *Rain* and *Wind*, in their function as supernatural agents, stand for fertility and growth, and "give life (motion)."[10]

> She moved under him, her rhythm merging into the sound of the wind shaking the rafters and the sound of the rain in the tree. And he was lost somewhere, deep beneath the surface of his own body and consciousness, swimming away from all his life before that hour (C 99).

Like all supernaturals, Night Swan is timeless and immortal. She "did not look old or young to him then; she was like the rain and the wind; age had no relation to her" (C 98). The sentence links Night Swan to Ts'eh, echoing Tayo's later description of Ts'eh's house that "age had little relation to it" (C 183). Later, both Night Swan and Ts'eh are connected to Ts'eh's mythic home, the mountain, which "was standing high and clear; months and years had no relation to the colors of gray slate and yellow sandstone circling it" (C 220).

Night Swan is aware of the significance of Tayo's visit and his complete unawareness of the events unfolding around him. Being endowed with supernatural power, Night Swan immediately recognizes the mythic potential inherent in Tayo. She tells him, "You don't have to understand what is happening. But remember this day. You will recognize it later. You are part of it now" (C 100). Bringing him to the door she says, "Thank you for bringing the message." Not Josiah's message, as Tayo assumes, but the message that the ceremony is still alive and that he will play a major part in its continuation. Originally thought up by the medicine man Descheeny and the Mexican woman a long time ago, and now continued by Night Swan and Ts'eh, the ceremony is designed to combat evil forces and return the world to its original state of perfect balance.

At first glance, the ceremony takes on an unexpected and seemingly dead end turnabout when Tayo and his cousin Rocky get stationed on a Pacific Island fighting the Japanese. When Rocky is wounded, Tayo and another soldier carry him on a stretcher through the drenching rain. Tayo fears the rain because it is bothering Rocky's wound and turning the road to mud. Forgetting Josiah's warning that thunder and floods "are part of life too, like the sun and the sky. You don't swear at them" (C 46), Tayo curses the rain:

> When Tayo prayed on the long muddy road to the prison camp, it was for dry air, dry as a hundred years squeezed out of yellow sand, air to dry out the oozing wounds of Rocky's leg, to let the torn flesh and broken bones breathe, to clear the sweat that filled Rocky's eyes. . . . The sound of the rain got louder . . . and the sound echoed inside his skull. . . . He damned the rain until [his] words were a chant, and he sang it while he crawled through the mud . . . (C 11-12).

Both Pueblos and Navajos believe that a curse like this can have serious consequences. "The power of the word," Reichard writes, "is as strong for evil as for good, an inverse wish being a curse."[11] And indeed, what directly follows Tayo's "praying against the rain" (C 12), is the mythical explanation for the subsequent drought. The Laguna myth of *Corn Woman* who scolded her sister, *Reed Woman*, for bathing while she was working in the sun, provides the mythic parallel to Tayo's curse. When *Corn Woman* got angry at her sister, *Reed Woman* went away to

> the original place
> down below
>
> And there was no more rain then.
> Everything dried up
>
> all the plants
> the corn
> the beans
> they all dried up
> and started blowing away
> in the wind.
>
> The people and the animals
> were thirsty.
> They were starving (C 13-14).

Following the myth, the narrative again picks up in New Mexico after the war: "So he had prayed the rain away and for the sixth year it was dry; the grass turned yellow and it did not grow. Wherever he looked, Tayo could see the consequences of his praying" (C 14). Laguna, once a place of water like the Place-of-Emergence, is presently an arid wasteland. Although emotionally disturbed, Tayo is still sufficiently in touch with the nature of mythic life to recognize the significance of his curse. Yet, although the course of the ceremony begun earlier seems interrupted, it soon becomes clear that, once chosen, Tayo will be guarded and guided back by the finely spun threads which pull him towards shipap, the ceremonial center of the Pueblo world.

The memories of disaster and destruction, combined with his guilt feelings about Rocky's death and the drought, cause Tayo to have a nervous breakdown. His emotional instability is mirrored in the spiritual disequilibrium experienced by his tribe. Tayo's "personal breakdown," Ruppert points out, "reflects the breakdown of Laguna cultural integrity. His personal dryness of emotion, spirit, and communal identity find physical manifestation in the drought suffered by the people of Laguna."[12] Like in Abel's case, white doctors and white medicines are unable to substitute for the emotional losses suffered. To the same extent that the Relocation Program was incapable of dealing with Abel's emotional problems, the VA hospital in California is incapable of helping Tayo overcome his confusion. He repeatedly experiences bodily dissociation and imagines himself invisible:

> For a long time he had been white smoke. He did not realize that until he left the hospital, because white smoke had no consciousness of itself. It faded into the white world of their bed sheets and walls; it was sucked away by the words of doctors who tried to talk to the invisible scattered smoke. He had seen outlines of gray steel tables, outlines of the food they pushed into his mouth, which was only an outline too, like all the outlines he saw (C 14).

Even more damaging than the war is the destruction of traditional tribal beliefs. A harsh characterization of an alienated woman appears in Tayo's aunt Thelma who is portrayed as a distant and cold Catholic. Having turned her back on the old ways, she fully abides by the laws of Christianity, a belief that "separated people from themselves; it tried to crush the single clan name, encouraging each person to stand alone, because Jesus Christ would save only the individual soul" (C 68). She has always been proud of her son Rocky whom she had encouraged to assimilate, believing he would achieve fame in the white man's world. Having abandoned the tribal rituals and with it the Pueblos' matrifocal foundation, Thelma had focused on her son Rocky as her sole source for status and approval, her only avenue to material and social advantage. She is the prototype of the stoic, assimilated woman who offers no spiritual connection to the past. With her son dead she delves even deeper into Christianity, seeking consolation in the promises of a better life thereafter.

Worst off are those who for a time had been integrated into the mainstream of society, the veterans who had been praised as patriotic Americans, only to be forgotten after the war. Trying to drown their bitterness, they use their disability checks to get drunk. Telling themselves that they had been the best soldiers in the U.S. Army, they curse the Whites whose war they had fought and for whom they had died "defending the land they had already lost" (C 169). Tayo's war buddies turn directly against their Pueblo heritage when they curse the much revered "Mother Earth," calling her an "old dried-up thing" (C 25). They blame others for the neglected ceremonies, for the lost stories, and for the abandoned beliefs in powers greater than the death, destruction, and displacement they had experienced in wartime. To them, the Fifth World seems to be altogether devoid of supernatural guidance.

Tayo tries to deceive himself by observing "how easy it was to stay alive now that he didn't care" (C 39); Ku'oosh, however, a Laguna medicine man, knows that being human requires both energy and responsibility. "A ceremony is required," writes Wiget, "to reintegrate Tayo's self by reimpressing upon his fragmented psyche the whole mythic pattern of the culture hero and his quest, thus restoring the shape of his personal and communal history and reestablishing his identity."[13] Since the Laguna elders believe that Tayo is in desperate need of a traditional ceremony designed to relieve signs of contact with dead enemies, they send him to Betonie, a Navajo healer. He is a rather unconventional medicine man who lives in the hills overlooking the Gallup ceremonial grounds, the place where the dark side of Native American existence is most visible. Tayo's life describes an ironic circle: his emotional recovery starts where his physical existence once began--among the prostitutes and their customers in the back alleys of Gallup. Although he initially mistrusts Betonie, Tayo soon finds comfort in one aspect they both share: Betonie's eyes "were hazel like his own" (C 119). Betonie explains that his grandmother "'was a remarkable Mexican with green eyes'" (C 119). His grandfather, Descheeny, also a medicine man, married the girl who had run away from her Mexican people. She had hidden among the trees and was given away by a "blue lace shawl" (C 147) that fell to the ground. Again, the color "blue" identifies her as a woman possessing mythic powers. It further links her to Night Swan who had surrounded herself with objects of blue, and to Ts'eh who also wears a blue shawl. And indeed, as Descheeny soon discovers, his Mexican wife is a mythical woman able to determine the course of history. "'He gazed into his smoky quartz crystal and she stared into the fire, and [together] they plotted the course of the ceremony," the ceremony which Tayo will conclude. (C 150-151).

When Tayo tells Betonie of his encounter with Night Swan, the medicine man is finally "beginning to see something . . . very important" (C 125). The similarity between the Mexican woman and Night Swan "prompts Betonie to understand Tayo's relationship to the ceremony planned by his grandparents."[14] Betonie realizes, like Night Swan before him, that Tayo has been selected to reenact the ceremony and reestablish his and his tribe's bond with the supernaturals. Surrounded by finely spun threads that pull him closer to the center where the creatrix resides, Tayo will experience the power of "time immemorial" and emerge as a healthy human being endowed with traditional knowledge and ritual power.

By the simple act of listening and encouraging him to speak of his war experiences, Betonie restores the memory that the white doctors' medicine had tried to drain out of Tayo. Betonie also tells him to follow his innermost feelings and accept the fact that his fate is only part of the overall malaise destroying the land. Tayo, however,

> . . . wanted to yell at the medicine man, to yell the things the white doctors had yelled at him, that he had to think only of himself, and not about the others, that he would never get well as long as he used words like 'we' and 'us'. But he had known the answer all along, even while the white doctors were telling him he could get well and he was trying to believe them: medicine didn't work that way, because the world didn't work that way. His sickness was only part of something larger, and his cure would be found only in something great and inclusive of everything (C 125-126).

Betonie counters Tayo's accusations against whites by reminding him that *Ts'its'tsi'nako* had created them all. Hating whites mirrors and feeds the Native Americans' own misery, or, as Betonie says, "you don't write off all the white people, just like you don't trust all Indians" (C 128). Furthermore, the utter desolation Tayo and others feel is not new. A hundred years ago the holy men saw that with the arrival of the white man "the balance of the world had been disturbed," and as a result, there would be "droughts and harder days to come" (C 186). In order to make Tayo see that he can master his fate and "deal with white people, with their machines and their beliefs" (C 132), Betonie presents Tayo with a story relating how Native Americans had invented the whites.[15]

The particular cure Betonie gives Tayo, the bear cure, is only the first step in an elaborate healing ritual. Tayo, like Abel and Set before him, must consciously experience and participate in the healing power of old myths. Only through the reenactment of mythic events can Tayo reach the state of wholeness and balance necessary to help him overcome his despair. A boy named Shush, meaning bear, the Pueblo animal-spirit of warriors and healers, is Betonie's helper. As a child Shush had spent some time with bears; hence,

Tayo notices "something strange about the boy, something remote in his eyes, as if he were on a distant mountaintop alone and the fire and hogan and the lights of the town below them did not exist" (C 128).

Betonie performs the Hoop Transformation Rite, and a Sandpainting of the Bear's Den ritual for Tayo. Whereas both the Night Chant as well as the Mountain Chant (from House Made of Dawn and The Ancient Child), belong to the category "good" (emphasis on the transformation from neutral to sacred, and on the attraction of good), the Hoop Transformation Rite belongs to the category "evil" (designed to both exorcise native ghosts and cure diseases caused by them, and to combat the effects of witchcraft):[16]

> A sandpainting is made, surrounded by a low bank of earth, or merely a circular ridge of sand and earth, open to the east, about two feet in diameter to enclose a space which is sprinkled with cornmeal. Spruce tree tops are stuck around it to form a sort of bower in which the patient sits. A person dressed as a bear, covered with branches of spruce, springs out from behind a blanket curtain or a dark corner of the hogan as if to terrify the patient.[17]

While Shush, the impersonator of Bear and thus the restoring force in the rite reenacts his part in Tayo's curing ceremony, Betonie starts the sandpainting--but with the dark color in the east. Wyman mentions that the normal sequence in a sandpainting is "the east, south, west, north [sunwise] sequence" with their corresponding colors "white, blue, yellow, black." If the colors "white" and "black" are exchanged (like in the case of Tayo's sandpainting), the arrangement "represents protection from danger coming from that quarter [east] and often is used in paintings of dangerous . . . events."[18] Aware of the next step in Tayo's healing ritual, Betonie thus protects him from any possible danger awaiting him around Mt. Taylor, located at some distance **east** of Gallup.

The sandpainting is an essential part of Navajo healing ceremonials. It "helps the patient," writes Zolbrod, "to 'emerge' from the locus of his illness back into the world which, dangerous as it is, can be kept orderly and controlled" (Diné 351). Just as he had to leave an opening in the sandpainting for evil spirits to get out, Betonie, by "cut[ting] Tayo across the top of his head" (C 143) with a sharp flint, gives the forces that are plaguing Tayo's body and mind a means to escape. By consciously participating in a healing ceremony, Tayo has undertaken the first step towards restoring balance (health) to himself as well as to his entire tribe. With his sandpainting, Betonie has achieved two major goals: he has significantly furthered Tayo's healing process; at the same time, he has provided desperately needed protection for Tayo's future encounters with dangerous forces.

After the completion of both the Hoop Transformation Rite and the sandpainting, Tayo "dreamed about the specked cattle" (C 145), a dream which according to traditional belief tells of supernatural guidance, thus "automatically bring[ing] good fortune."[19] With the ceremonies performed and the stories told, Betonie sends Tayo on his way to find both Josiah's lost cattle and his own lost identity. Betonie is aware that the ceremony "lay to rest the Japanese souls in the green humid jungles, and [that] it satisfied the female giant who fed on the dreams of warriors." But he also realizes that "there was something else now" (C 169), something even more important to the successful completion of the entire ceremony. He reminds Tayo of the four tasks he still needs to complete: "Remember the stars," Betonie says, "I've seen them and I've seen the spotted cattle; I've seen a mountain and I've seen a woman" (C 152).

In the beginning of the novel Tayo personified qualities of the east, for instance, in his "guise as 'white smoke;' in the genetic 'blood' of his unknown white father; in the way the Laguna assign white people to the east, including the Japanese who inhabit the land of the rising sun. . . ."[20] At Night Swan's place Tayo then gets in touch with the color blue, the sacred color of the

West, and he experiences *Bear*, the sacred animal of the West, in Betonie's mountains. Blue, the color that had surrounded both Descheeny's wife as well as Night Swan, is also abundantly present everywhere in nature as Tayo makes his way towards Tse'pina, Mt. Taylor. Tse'pina's blue color that Tayo had already noticed at Betonie's place (C 128), is joined by the blue of the sky, the clouds, the flowers, the stones, and the rain. The intricate web of color, animal, and directional symbolism that had surrounded Tayo all along, intensifies as he makes his way towards the holy mountain of the Keres.

Approaching Tse'pina in the north, yellow takes over as the sacred color, and *Mountain Lion*, sacred hunter of the north, rules as the prime animal. Ts'eh, the woman of Night Swan's dreams and Betonie's vision, wears "a yellow skirt" and has "light brown skin" and "ocher eyes" (C 177). These features link her to the Pueblo goddess complex of *Yellow Woman*, both a mountain spirit with yellow face and the generic term for mythic heroines of Laguna stories.[21] Another link to *Yellow Woman* is Silko's own description of this mythical woman as having "light hair and eyes" in her short story "Yellow Woman."[22] It is further likely that Ts'eh is *Yellow Woman* since "the Acoma-Laguna stories concerning her are located on or around Mount Taylor. . . ."[23] The Keres see *Yellow Woman* as goddess of the game and giver of place-names. Zolbrod mentions the importance of naming, saying that supernaturals "assert their leadership as creators by speaking out and naming places and things, which is something like mapping an entire culture" (Dinė 356). Ts'eh is further the initial homophone in two crucial Laguna words: *Ts'its'tsi'nako*, *Thought Woman*, and Tse'pina, Mount Taylor, the holy mountain of the Laguna.

Myths recount *Spider Woman*'s creation and placing of the sacred mountains in each cardinal direction, the zenith, and the nadir. Since mountains are considered the homes of the supernaturals, people in the lower worlds "took special care to bring tokens of the mountains with them"[24] when floods forced them to leave. Ts'eh introduces herself as "a Montano" (C 223), a Mountain

Woman. When Tayo asks her about her family she looks "towards the Black Mountains in the south" (C 223), saying that one sister lives south, one near Flagstaff, and one brother in Jemez. These locations coincide with the other sacred mountains of the Pueblo universe. Ts'eh inhabits Mt. Taylor; San Francisco Peak (called Navajo Mountain by the Navajos) is located near Flagstaff; San Miguel Mountain is just outside Jemez, and south of Mt. Taylor are the sacred Black Mountains.

Ts'eh's first words, "Somebody sent you" (176), establish her as a woman endowed with visionary power. Tayo soon realizes Ts'eh's mythic stature and understands that "like old Betonie, she could see reflections in sandrock pools of rainwater, images shifting in the flames of juniper fire, she heard voices, low and distant in the night" (C 232). Tayo's quest north to the Keres place of mythic origin offers a mythical place of healing. Like Lukachukai for Set, Tse'pi'na grants Tayo a measure of natural calmness and enables him to gather the strength he will need for the completion of the ceremony.

Ts'eh "was holding a small willow staff, slightly curved on one end" (C 176). When he meets her again she "was walking through the sunflowers, holding the blue silk shawl around her shoulders in one hand, carrying the long curved willow stick in the other" (C 221). The "blue silk shawl" recalls "the blue lace shawl" Descheeny's wife had lost a century ago. The willow branch connects Ts'eh to Descheeny who customarily used a "walking cane" (C 148). The cane, as Reichard mentions, is "a symbol of great ritualistic power," since by either sticking it in the ground or drawing in the rain clouds with the crooked end, people are always assured of getting water.[25] Ts'eh is accompanied by *Arrow Youth, Hunter*, a brother or husband, friend of the Great Star. Like *Yellow Woman*, who wears her hair "pinned back in a knot" (C 177), he emphasizes the traditional ways, singing Pueblo songs, wearing "his hair long, tied back with white cotton string in the old style . . ." (C 207). *Arrow Youth* is normally accompanied by "the hunter's helper" (C 196), *Mountain Lion*, "the Katcina spirit who provides hunting techniques, and controls the capture of game in the north."[26] When Tayo first notices *Arrow Youth* approaching from the north, the hunter wears a cap "made from tawny thick fur [which] looked like mountain lion skin" (C 207). This cap links *Arrow Youth* to Descheeny who used to wear an "old badger fur hat" (C 148).

When Tayo enters Ts'eh's house he "touched a whitewashed wall as he went through a doorway, and rubbed the powdery clay between his fingers" (C 178). White clay, one of the ritual substances used in sandpaintings to drive away enemy ghosts,[27] functions as a further connection between the three women. The Mexican captive had inhabited a mountain overlooking the "white clay springs" (C 148), and Night Swan's room had "smelled like the white clay the people used for whitewash" (C 98). It was in her room that Tayo "picked up a fragment of fallen plaster and drew dusty white stripes across the backs of his hands, the way ceremonial dancers sometimes did, except they used white clay, and not old plaster" (C 104). Now, at Ts'eh's home, Tayo encounters for the first time white clay, not as plaster, but in its pure form. Similarly, he faces for the first time not a mystical woman able to see beyond the confines of physical reality, but a creatrix, a woman from "time immemorial," a woman able to both initiate and cultivate new existence. Since the time he had left Betonie he had watched the sky, "looking for the pattern of stars the old man drew on the ground that night." Now, during his first meeting with Ts'eh, he notices that "Old Betonie's stars were there" (C 178). The various parts of the ceremony, like an elaborate puzzle, are slowly beginning to come together.

Tayo's encounters with Ts'eh are of a dreamlike and somewhat mythical nature. She knows about him without asking and she possesses ephemeral qualities, appearing and disappearing suddenly. When they make love, "he felt her body, and it was warm as the sand, and he couldn't feel where her body ended and the sand began" (C 222). Merged with the sand, she is Earth herself; yet, in her function as the *Moon Mother* she is equally at home in the sky:

> She pulled herself to the top [and] the canyon and the rock of the cliff seemed suddenly gone as if [Tayo] had stepped from the earth into the sky; where they were, the sky was more than half the world; it enclosed the mesa top where they stood (C 223).

Whereas Ts'eh provides Tayo with the spiritual and emotional background necessary to withstand the witchery, *Mountain Lion*, Ts'eh's animal manifestation, supplies Tayo with physical protection. When Tayo encounters *Mountain Lion* he knows that even without Ts'eh's continued presence he is in her keeping. Lying on the ground, Tayo watches "the yellow form that moved toward [him]. . . ." He sees *Yellow Woman, Moon Mother* of the *War Twins*, in *Mountain Lion*'s eyes which "caught twin reflections of the moon." And when "the mountain lion stopped in front of him, it was not hesitation, but a chance for the moonlight to catch up with him." After *Mountain Lion* left, "his outline lingering like yellow smoke," Tayo "poured yellow pollen from Josiah's tobacco sack into the cup of his hand [and] sprinkled pinches of yellow pollen into the four footprints" (C 196). *Mountain Lion* is a very secretive and mysterious animal. As a powerful animal spirit, *Mountain Lion* possesses power for both curing and war. *Mountain Lion* fulfills his mythic role when the two Texan land guards decide to go after him rather than take Tayo to prison (C 202). With his sacred "weapons" hail, ice, and snow, that covered everything, "burying the mountain lion's tracks and obliterating his scent" (C 205), *Mountain Lion* manages to save both Tayo's life as well as its own.

During their time together, Ts'eh and Tayo are surrounded by "the yellows and the orange of the sandrock cliffs," while the earth is covered with "silky yellow petals like wild canary feathers, and blossoms as dark as the center of the sun" (C 220). Deeply in love with Ts'eh and surrounded by the color yellow, which among the Keres "is the color for women," Tayo "becomes conscious of the female side of his own nature and accepts and integrates feminine behavior into his life."[28] The reintegration of the feminine side of his personality becomes apparent in his reawakened interest in and care for nature: "He found flowers that had no bees, and gathered yellow pollen gently with a small blue feather from Josiah's pouch; he imitated the gentleness of the bees as they brushed their sticky-haired feet and bellies softly against the flowers" (C 220).

This re-opening of Tayo's lifeline to nature is further continued on Pa'to'ch, the high mesa he had seen in his dreams. When he finally finds his uncle's cattle there, he knows that "the dark earth loved him" (C 202), and that it is up to him to join her: "The magnetism of the center spread over him." It was "pulling him back, close to the earth" and even with "the noise and pain in his head he knew how it would be: a returning rather than a separation" (C 201). By entering into a bond with Ts'eh, the contemporary aspect of *Yellow Woman* and thus with Earth herself, Tayo acknowledges the existence of an ever-present mythical past.

Finally, Betonie's teachings become "a story he could feel happening - from the stars and the woman, the mountain and the cattle . . ." (C 186). Once Tayo experienced the validity of Betonie's prophecy, he is not only a conscious participant in the continuation of his story, but an active force in the development of the ceremony. When he sings the sunrise song *Yellow Woman*'s impact on Tayo becomes apparent:

> Being alive was all right then; he had not breathed like that for a long time. Coming closer to the river, faintly at first, faint as the pale yellow light emerging across the southeast horizon, the sound gathered intensity from the swelling colors of dawn. And at that moment, the sun came over the edge of the horizon, they suddeniy appeared on the riverbank, the Ka't'sina approaching the river crossing. He stood up. He knew the people had a song for the sunrise. . . . He repeated the words as he remembered them, not sure if they were the right ones, but feeling they were right, feeling the

> instant of the dawn was an event which in a single moment gathered all things together - the last stars, the mountaintops, the clouds, and the winds - celebrating this coming (C 181-182).

At Laguna, *Yellow Woman* is both the generic name for all female Ka't'sinas and for the "founding mother" of the Antelope Clan which originated in the Keresan speaking Acoma Pueblo.[29] Ts'eh, in her function as *Yellow Woman*, is also a Ka't'sina; her eyes and cheek bones slant upward suggesting the "face of an antelope dancer's mask" (C 177). Being closely associated with the Ka't'sina cult, Antelope is also an animal of great importance in ritual. Ts'eh's antelope features are linked to the spotted cattle which run like antelopes and are throughout compared to "desert antelope" (C 80, 74). This again links her to Night Swan who had originally urged Josiah to purchase the cattle. Similar to most of the characters in Ceremony who are mixed bloods (Tayo, Descheeny's wife, and Night Swan, for once), the spotted cattle "are not animals from traditional Pueblo mythology or storytelling tradition." Instead, Silko "created them to represent the hybridization of Indian culture."[30]

In the western Pueblos the Ka't'sinas are responsible for the relationship between people on the one side, and rain and the dead on the other. Tayo's morning prayer to the Ka't'sinas is thus meaningful on different levels: first, it tries to reverse his curse of the rain; second, the prayer reminds him that the deaths of Rocky and Josiah are supernaturally ordered facts and should therefore be devoid of any guilt feelings on his part; and lastly, by praying Tayo acknowledges Ts'eh in her function as leader of all Ka't'sinas, as "the Mother of us all." Tayo's song and prayer are reminiscent of Abel's race at the end of House Made of Dawn. Ostensibly alone, Tayo, like Abel, does not experience the moment as isolation. Like Momaday's protagonist, he suddenly remembers words that had not surfaced in his consciousness for a long time. Relying on intuitional knowledge and mythic vision, he senses the presence of the Ka't'sinas and knows that he is in touch with very fundamental life forces. Like with Abel towards the end of House Made of Dawn, the performative dimensions of the prayer act "serve its pragmatic concerns by engendering the powers of evocation which can transform moods, reshape motivations, muster courage, and present meaning-giving images." This means,

> that while prayer is the communication of an intelligible message describing an expected pragmatic effect, the form in which that message is carried engages real processes which serve to achieve the desired results, even to the extent of physical cure.[31]

Throughout the latter part of Ceremony, Silko emphasizes the healing function of Tayo's connection to Ts'eh. Since Ts'eh is *Kochinnenako, Yellow Woman,* she is eternal. As long as the stories are known and the ceremonies are followed, she will provide the physical as well as spiritual necessities of life. It is up to Tayo and others to seek her and her ways. "Ts'eh is the matrix, the creative and life-restoring power, and those who cooperate with her designs serve her and, through her, serve life."[32] Through Ts'eh, Tayo experiences the power of myths and realizes that nothing is lost if people remember "the stories of the creation and continuation of the five worlds . . ." (C 249). He can finally be certain that

> Josiah and Rocky were not far away. They were close; they had always been close. And he loved them then as he had always loved them, the feeling pulsing over him as strong as it had ever been. They loved him that way; he could still feel the love they had for him. The damage that had been done had never reached this feeling. This feeling was their life, vitality locked deep in blood memory, and the people were strong, and the fifth world endured, and nothing was ever lost as long as the love remained (C 219-220).

Even back at his aunt's place, Ts'eh is ever-present. Every morning "he would wake up at the first dim light with the presence and the feeling that she had been with him all night." For the first time in his life he feels loved and in return, he is "overwhelmed by the love he felt for her" (C 215, 217-218). He also realizes that "she had always loved him, she had never left him; she had always been there" (C 255). Like Angela and Grey, Ts'eh knows the "story," the mythic plan, the protagonist needs to follow. And like Abel and Set before him, Tayo needs to remember and act according to the story. Ts'eh warns Tayo never to forget the story. Not just the story of two people, but the story of creation, the story of *Yellow Woman* and her design. "As long as you remember, it is part of this story we have together," she tells him (C 231). Like Abel and Set, Tayo experiences his connection to tribal mythology through both his relationship to a mythological woman-figure and his participation in a mythic story.

Not even his friends are able to weaken his newly won convictions. Observing their self-destructive behavior, Tayo recalls just in time Ts'eh's warning that "they" - presumably all not possessing Pueblo wisdom - want to end his story. He has the strength not to join in their self-annihilation because he knows that to abide by the power of hatred and death is to surrender to witchery. Instead, confident from his experience with Ts'eh that larger powers are at work, Tayo relinquishes all thoughts of entering into their violent games. "A sense of ceremony, restored to Tayo, also instills positive abstinence, knowing what *not* to do." Tayo's nonaction, "the wise patience, the discipline, the informed waiting [is] counseled by the care of ceremonial design.[33] This is the way to resist despair and to bring native life back into balance. Reichard agrees, writing that "it is as important to know what to omit and why as to know what to include. Knowledge, therefore, is the power derived through a long and involved process of learning divulged by the myths."[34] When his friends eventually die or leave, Tayo knows that witchery has rebounded upon itself.

As the leaders of the Pueblo had hoped, Tayo's purification and healing provide for the renewal and continuance of his community despite the wounds of the present generation. Tayo has reached the end of his ceremony, and he can now tell the holy men in the kiva what he has learned:

> He cried the relief he felt at finally seeing the pattern, the way all the stories fit together - the old stories, the war stories, their stories - to become the story that was still being told. He was not crazy; he had never been crazy. He had only seen and heard the world as it always was: no boundaries, only transitions through all distances and time (C 246).

Since for the tribe the loss of *Yellow Woman* "portends loss of rain, of livelihood, and of connection between the people and the sacred place where Iyatiku lives, Shipap,"[35] Tayo's linkage with *Yellow Woman* assures rain, growth, and the continuity of tribal life. The Pueblo's shattered connection to the spirit world is now reestablished, and they know the drought will end:

> In *Ceremony* . . . the problem of healing is multidimensional. First of all, the afflicted person must be dealt with; second, the land itself manifests the illness, so the drought must be dealt with. Third, because the illness of one tribal member contaminates the whole tribe, the cure must be all-inclusive. Fourth, the mind and body of the sick person . . . can be cured only by simultaneously healing the spirit.[36]

Silko juxtaposes the happy ending of Tayo, his land, and his people, with the happy ending of the myths that she had interspersed all along. Whereas the seductions of witchery are the models of those like Tayo's former friends who live on the dying of others, it is the *Earth Woman/Yellow Woman* figures - the Mexican captive, Night Swan, and ultimately and most importantly, Ts'eh - who are working for rain, healing, fertility, and Tayo's restoration.

At the point of Tayo's return to tribal tradition the land blooms again, and the "valley was green, from the yellow sandstone mesas in the northwest to the black lava hills to the south" (C 219). When Ts'eh asks him to gather the plant that contains the "light of the stars, and the moon penetrating the night" (C 227), she asks him to take on her duties as earth's nurturing force. By his willingness to sow and care for Ts'eh's plants, he joins Earth, the matrix, and participates in her all-encompassing design.

Alfonso Ortiz states that "a Pueblo priest, when setting out a dry painting, will first carefully set out the boundaries and then work his way *inward* toward the center. The Navajo singer, on the other hand, will work *outward* from the middle."[37] Consequently, the Pueblo belief that only a healthy society brings forth well-balanced individuals stands in sharp contrast to Momaday's philosophy based on the Navajo belief that a well-balanced individual is the prerequisite of a functioning tribal existence. The healing process according to Pueblo ways **has** to start with a ceremony which is all-inclusive, directed towards the general common good. Since Tayo's recovery is desirable mainly in that it directly relates to the well-being of the tribe as a whole--thereby far superceding the individual quest of Momaday's protagonists--Silko's novel promises a more complete transformation of Native American society. As Ruppert says, "Ts'eh's ceremony is Tayo's path to reintegration back to identity on the personal, cultural, and mythic level. But it is also the Laguna path back to reintegration. . . ." It is doubtful that Ruppert is correct by continuing the above phrase, "and ultimately, the world's,"[38] since Ceremony solely focuses on Pueblo society. Only Betonie (significantly a Navajo healer) does not support the perpetrator/victim attitude and thus represents a world view that would warrant a belief in the all-inclusiveness Ruppert seems to perceive.

Tayo is a rather reluctant and passive protagonist. Never the one to initiate action, he is--without at first realizing it--being pushed and pulled towards the ceremony's successful conclusion. By de-emphasizing the significance of the protagonist's thoughts and actions and focusing instead on the importance of a supernaturally ordered system to revive Pueblo society, Silko once more affirms her groundedness in the Pueblo storyteller tradition. Not individual action by an overarching hero, but communal remembering, creating, and following a mythic story ultimately defeats evil and celebrates life.

Like the trinity of goddesses in Keresan mythology (*Ts'its'tsi'nako*, *Naotsete*, and *Uretsete*), three powerful women endowed with supernatural abilities are either by association (the Mexican), or physically/spiritually (Night Swan, Ts'eh) connected to Tayo. As the last and most powerful in this chain of mythic female characters, Ts'eh is ultimately responsible for the successful completion of the ceremony. Interconnected by their mythical power and surrounded by an elaborate code of color, animal, and directional symbolism, this female thread of characters provides Tayo with his cultural and mythic identity. As opposed to Momaday's male protagonists whose deeds and thoughts determine much of the novels' development, Ceremony is held together by an elaborate network of female characters who spread out like a spider's web to cover the fabric of a matrifocal society.

V.

Paula Gunn Allen[1]

Ephanie and Spider Woman

The Woman Who Owned the Shadows - And Still Does

> She had dreamed one night of a grey-striped kitten that in the dream had been skinned by Teresa's Colorado friends. The pitiful little thing had bled, its bare flesh pink and oozing. But it had roused itself and walked to its dish. It had begun calmly to eat (WOS 147).

Paralleling the structure of Momaday's novels, Paula Gunn Allen's The Woman Who Owned the Shadows is divided into four parts (again reflecting the Navajo/Pueblo holy number). Each part is preceded by a prologue recounting a mythological event. Like Silko, Allen dedicates her novel to "Spider Grandmother, Thought Woman, who thinks the stories I write down" (WOS, foreword). Unlike the main characters discussed prior, Allen's protagonist is a woman; at the date of its publication, The Woman Who Owned the Shadows was "the first novel written *by* an American Indian woman *about* an Indian woman published in the last 50 years."[2] In the novel, dreams, events, mythic tales, Native American as well as personal history, and internal dialogue all run together, creating a non-linear, non-sequential narrative structure.

Whereas Momaday and Silko describe life on the reservation as at least containing the possibility of a functioning and supportive organism, Allen's protagonist hardly finds any understanding within her tribal community. As opposed to the novels previously discussed, in which complete well-being for a Native American seemed to be possible only outside of white industrial settlements and within the protective confines of reservation life, Ephanie's final reattachment to the ways of the past is not linked to any tribal location. By turning her protagonist into a modern, western-style educated woman living in the big city, Allen, more than the other novelists, emphasizes the **current** appeal of mythological tales--their ability to cross the boundaries of religion, ethnicity, and color. And whereas Momaday and Silko chose women to provide the protagonist with the emotional, spiritual, and sexual support necessary to master his fate, Allen created a female protagonist who finds emotional stability only after relinquishing all relationships with men. As opposed to the other protagonists who have to learn to trust unconditionally, Ephanie has to learn to rely on herself and to be suspicious of other people's motives. After relinquishing all relationships, Ephanie is ready to go on the archetypal journey of departure, initiation, and return.

The great works on the hero--such as Joseph Campbell's The Hero with a Thousand Faces--all start out with the assumption that the hero-protagonist is male. This bias has given the impression that in literature (and thus probably in life) heroism is an entirely male phenomenon. The portrait of Ephanie in The Woman Who Owned the Shadows clearly demonstrates that the denial of female courage and assertiveness results in a psychological imprisonment hard to escape.

As opposed to the three novels previously discussed, which all are structured according to native chantways, Ephanie essentially follows in the footsteps of Campbell's three archetypal stages. In Part I of the novel, she departs from everything known to her; Part II and III constitute the psychological journey during which she slays the inner dragons of insecurity and apparent powerlessness; Part IV focuses on her spiritual "home-coming." Instead of simply rejoicing in her newly won internal balance at that point, however, she will first have to confront the external dragons of patriarchal society.

Like Abel, Set, and Tayo, Ephanie suffers from emotional problems so overwhelming that her only response consists in her complete withdrawal from life. "At the center of Paula Gunn Allen's vision," writes Elizabeth Hanson, "is an individual alienated within."[3] Like the other protagonists she sometimes wonders if she really exists: "I didn't have that conversation with Stephen. I wonder if I can speak at all. To anyone" (WOS 5). Somehow sensing that her life has gone awry, she is trying to figure out how she can escape her immanent emotional paralysis. Her initial difficulty, like that of Abel, Tayo, and Set, is finding a point of entry into the ritual pattern of her people. Yet, whereas the male protagonists had a female aiding them in the process of uncovering the mythic reality of life, Ephanie is solely searching within herself for the answers in an oftentimes painful and self-destructive manner.

Devastated by an unsuccessful marriage and an unfaithful husband who abandoned her and their two children, Ephanie is unable to relate to either friends or relatives. She tries to escape Pueblo life by moving with Agnes and Ben to San Francisco, "somewhere west of where she lived. Somewhere west of yesterday" (WOS 46). Ephanie feels drawn towards the West which, as symbol, is indicative of "a highly sacred or powerful vision and signif[ies] revelation, introspection, and deep change." Due to these qualities, the West is "said to be terrifying because [it has] the power to 'make live' and the power to destroy."[4] The image of "predawn waves" (WOS 46) points toward the flooded lowest world, and thus to "shipap," the Place-of-Emergence, the "place that first and finally is home" (WOS 130). Returning to "shipap," Ephanie descends into the underworld of her psyche to encounter the life-denying forces of self-loathing, fear, and paralysis. San Francisco, or the West Coast in general, thus serves as the place that forces Ephanie to confront the "dragons within." The move enables her to go on the psychological journey in search of her true self and escape the captivity of her conditioning. Following the archetypal stages of the heroine's journey as described in The Female Hero, Ephanie's descent "is depicted as a retreat into a state of temporary madness; as an adventure in the world of dreams."[5]

> In the first stage, the hero exits from the garden when she comes to realize that people she had previously seen as guides for her life - parents, husbands, religious or political authorities - are her captors.

> To free herself, she must leave the garden of dependency and the captor figures, slay the dragon of the virginity myth, and assume the role of spiritual orphan. Her treasure at this stage is freedom and unlimited possibility.[6]

Ephanie's development from a woman devastated by life to an integrated and balanced human being becomes manifest through various symbols, the most important one being the sun symbolism. It figures prominently in the "current events" part of the novel as well as in Ephanie's flashback memories. Through "sun," one of the most paramount symbols in southwestern mythology, the various episodes that helped shape Ephanie's life acquire new dimensions. More importantly, *Sun*, the most highly regarded male god in southwestern myths and father of the *War Twins*, will help her discover the existence of her mythical counterpart, *Spider Woman*.

On a superficial level Ephanie's problems seem to stem from her half-breed status that makes her an outsider everywhere she goes. Like Abel and Tayo, Ephanie is a half-breed; unlike them, she considers her half-breed status the overwhelming problem in her life. At the beginning of the novel, Ephanie is aware of the deep fragmentation accompanying every aspect of her existence:

> Ephanie. Too strange a name, deranging her from the time she first understood its strangeness. Her body, choppy and short, sturdy, was at odds with her name. Ephanie was for someone tall and serene. Someone filled with grace. But like her it was a split name, a name half of this and half of that: Epiphany. Effie. An almost name. An almost event. Proper at that for her, a halfblood. A halfbreed. Which was the source of her derangement (WOS 3).

Her present life which is filled with nothing but "walking, aimless, around the room, sniffing, looking dogwise for some clue" (WOS 5-6), is juxtaposed with earlier, happier times:

> She had dreamed . . . of herself with Elena, amiga, tiny girls, running in frantic circles around her grandmother's house, screaming. Being chased by a long circle of animals: coyotes and wolves, bear, and deer, antelope and jackrabbits, goats and lizards, snakes. Running forever with no way to escape while the others - mother and aunts, sisters and grandmother stood, watched, slouching familiarly with each other, laughing and pointing. Unconcerned (WOS 6).

The world seems perfect and undisturbed. The Native American circle, the "sacred hoop" of existence, is complete and provides safety. Women figure in the foreground, the oral traditions are alive, stories take on shape, animals of midwinter tales appear. What, then, has happened in these roughly thirty years that have elapsed since her grandmother's house was the center of the universe? What has happened to the once self-assured, strong Ephanie?

The answer appears in her thoughts throughout the novel, most often when Stephen is around. She feels that people, more specifically, men, have taken over her life, are still taking over her very being. As Stephen, her life-long friend, assures her: "You are new, Ephanie. I have remade you" (WOS 17). She constantly feels the need to correct something, to "undo what he had done" (WOS 11), yet, she is incapable of specifying exactly what it is. Ephanie's dilemma represents Native American history: "Long before, they had taken everything away," she muses. And "they knew a lot about [freedom] because . . . they were free to do anything they wanted to somebody else" (Wos 20). When she remembers the history of her ancestors, painful memories of the Ghost Dance movement and **Wounded Knee** surface:

> In the last days they painted their faces black and shuffled circlewise, hands locking. . . . They saw the ones they had lost and were comforted for awhile. Eating pemmican. Rose, danced again. Soot blackened faces howling toward the sky. And lost again. Were lost.

> Blood frozen in the snow. Finality. He said a dream had died there. He was not wrong (WOS 47).

At one point Native American history and her own personal dilemma start to converge. They want to "take control of her very breath. To tell her when and how to breathe. He was" (WOS 19). As becomes clear with the novel's progression, Ephanie's search, unlike that of the other protagonists, is prompted not so much by a yearning for **ethnic** acceptance within the tribal structure, but by the need for a **sexual** identity within her own personal self.

In flashback scenes Ephanie remembers the first painful experience of her life. In her reveries of that specific day, *Sun* is no longer perceived as the benevolent keeper of time and determining aspect of the seasons, but instead as a powerfully cruel and dominating force. At the beginning of that day, *Sun* "was high and the earth around them looked flat. Sunbitten" (WOS 27). While the two friends, Ephanie and Elena, were lying "at peace" in the alfalfa field, *Sun* made "promises it would never keep" (WOS 22). When her girlfriend Elena told her that they could not see each other anymore since the nuns said that all the "hugging and giggling . . . was the devil," Ephanie felt the "enormity of the abyss she was falling into. The endless, endless depth of the void" (WOS 30). And *Sun*, instead of trying to soften the blow, "was blazing down on them, unconcerned" (WOS 29). After losing her friend, the pots she made out of "useless yellow clay" were only for *Sun* "to eat" (WOS 82).

Ephanie is initially unable to remember two more incidents in her life that negatively influenced her in her development as a woman. She senses, however, that both events are tied to Stephen, "her teacher, her guide, her loving friend, her strength . . ." (WOS 15). Instead of strong emotions, all she gets are glimpses "so far behind memory and so easily confused with dream" (WOS 21):

> She remembered something. That had no words, That had no pictures. About Stephen, the light. The heat of that July day. The sun blazing, hurting her head, stupifying [sic] her brain. The numbing sun. The fire. A shadow coming down over her. A hand. A mouth. A feeling of suffocation. On her chest heavy. Knowing that she would surely die. Wanted to. But that she could not remember (WOS 14).

Since Ephanie has only dim memories of the rape, the only glimpse at her devastating experience is provided through her notion of *Sun*'s light which she perceives as treacherous, feeling that it aided in her victimization. Completing the series of devastations is Ephanie's fall from an apple-tree at the age of twelve. Stephen had prompted her to swing from a tree; after she fell she "didn't say much except that she was sorry. That she shouldn't have done that [and that] she should have listened . . . to all of them, to their warnings, to their fear, to their complaints." Her life changes after the fall: "How she dressed. How she walked. What she thought. Where she went. How she spoke. The old ease with her body was gone" (WOS 202).

In contrast to the previous protagonists, the alienation she feels is due not so much to her halfblood status, her withdrawal from the land of her forebears, or any wars in the white man's world, but to the fall from the tree which she considered her due punishment for the inexplicable sexual molestation she had suffered prior. Ephanie is the victim of sexual abuse; at the same time, she also falls victim to a structure of patriarchal values. Having felt fear, shame, and insecurity, Ephanie now internalizes the concept of "sin." As a consequence, she abandons her former Native American belief system and adopts the view of female sinfulness.

"Ephanies Fall vom Apfelbaum," says Zwillus, "[ist] eine symbolische Wiederholung des christlichen Sündenfalls."[7] Ephanie is familiar with Christian thought since her grandfather, a white man, was a Christian. Also, while largely abiding by their gynocratic perspective, the Pueblos have nevertheless incorporated both Christian and male dominant views into their tribal structure due to the long-standing presence of Christian missionaries. Perceiving herself a "fallen woman," Ephanie now devotes herself to the teachings of Christianity, hoping to be cleansed of her sin:

> After she fell she had begun rising early to attend morning Mass. Had given up grandiose dreams for Lent. Had forgotten how to spin dreams, imaginings about her life, her future self, her present delights. Had cut herself off from the sweet spring of her own being. Bless me father for I have sinned. But I won't sin anymore, she vowed. Had learned piety and modesty (WOS 203).

Ephanie does not only adhere to the superficial aspects of the Christian faith, but internalizes some views of Christianity, most importantly, the Christian view of women. She feels that she, like Eve, the first woman of Christianity and female prototype in Christian societies, is being chased out of Eden for her sin. She assumes the view of original female sinfulness, as proclaimed in the Old Testament, and from now on her life will bear the stamp of female guilt. In her subsequent encounters with men, Ephanie will forever try to undo her sin. Mary Daly explains the theological basis for this voluntary self-sacrifice on the part of women in <u>Beyond God the Father</u>:

> The qualities that Christianity **idealizes**, especially for women, are also those of a victim: sacrificial love, passive acceptance of suffering, humility, meekness [and] since women cannot be "good" enough to measure up to this ideal . . . this is an impossible model. Thus doomed to failure even in emulating the Victim, women are plunged more deeply into victimization.[8]

After her fall from the tree, the formerly tomboyish Ephanie is suddenly filled with fear and the awareness that not everything is within her reach. Like most of her peers, she turns into a girl solely occupied with lacy dresses and high heels. She learns "to prance and priss, and did not notice the change, the fear behind it. The rage. And did not ever say aloud, not even in her own mind, what it was all about" (WOS 203).

"After she fell the sun went out" (WOS 203). After her fall from the apple-tree, Ephanie blames the "bright, the pitiless, the unwavering sun" (WOS 23) for the accident. All the pain "of the dead and the dying, the longing-to-be-born, the mercilessly hating, the loathing-the-self" is always and everywhere surrounded by "the pouring liquid sun . . . (WOS 96). *Sun*, once the central issue, the keeper of seasons in the Pueblos, is now replaced by the mechanical chronology of obligatory prayers and church attendances. From now on Ephanie will be denying "all she knew and based her life upon," completely negating "her one true heart" (WOS 98).

Since the time of that accident, Ephanie has struggled with her female identity and encountered a multitude of obstacles on her way to womanhood; it is therefore important to analyze the novel from the added perspective of feminism. Ephanie vacillates between "being dependent and strong, self-reliant and powerless, strongly motivated and hopelessly insecure."[9] Having to identify with two hopelessly opposed cultural definitions of women, Ephanie feels that she now collides with the structure of patriarchal society which defines female independent behavior as "theologically evil, biologically unnatural, psychologically unhealthy, and socially in bad taste."[10]

Ephanie is afraid to remember. She actively tries to escape her past, not realizing that in the process she avoids her only chance for recovery--her people's myths. "And taking the broom [she] vacuumed up the webs, spiders and all" (WOS 34). By killing the spider, thus symbolically disregarding *Spider Woman*, the creator being of the Pueblos and the Native American gynocratic spirit, Ephanie consciously cuts herself off from both her mythic background and her female identity. Her dissention from Keres traditionalism becomes apparent in her thought processes. As opposed to *Spider Woman* who thinks things into existence, Ephanie thinks about them after they have happened. "[Stephen] put down his cup. Picked up his jacket and put it on. Pick up the jacket, Stephen, she thought. Put it on" (WOS 44).

Ephanie is a highly discontent, deeply fragmented human being. She finds consolation neither in the Pueblo nor in the white or Native American community in San Francisco. She attacks people on all sides: whites who stole the land and brought in Christianity, whites who criticize their forefathers for destroying the natives' lifeways, and natives who dwell on their role as impotent victims rather than finding ways to improve their situation. For Ephanie, nothing is simple: "What do you do," she asks, "when you love everybody on every side of the war" (WOS 146)? Slashing out against virtually all people on either side of the argument, Ephanie is initially destroying herself in the process. To the same extent that she sees Native Americans accept their fate as a given and unchangeable fact, she realizes her own paralysis which she blames on her half-breed status within an all native or all white community. Teresa, a white woman with the ability to foretell the future, gives Ephanie the first inkling of her eventual salvation:

> "The thing is that [the spirits] want you to know that someone is watching out for you. She's an older woman with white hair. She wears a particular pin on her dress, it's a small turquoise and silver one, shaped like a spider. She wears thick glasses and she's smiling and nodding. Do you recognize her?" (WOS 62).

Much later Ephanie "remembered the pin her grandmother had worn, the one that looked like a spider with a pale blue body" (WOS 98). Although Teresa foreshadows the source of Ephanie's ultimate liberation--*Grandmother Spider*--Ephanie is still too alienated from the traditional myths and beliefs to recognize the significance of Teresa's predictions.

Out of loneliness and pity Ephanie marries Thomas Yoshuri, a Japanese-American from the 'land of the rising sun'. She thereby enters the second stage of the heroine's journey where the "powerful figure is the seducer." However, he "turns out to be another captor," and the hero finds she must "slay the dragon of romantic love and demythologize the seducer."[11] Continuing on her archetypal journey, Ephanie indeed leaves Thomas shortly after their marriage and, like *Sun*'s wife *Kochinnenako*, bears twin sons. When one of the twins dies, she buries him in the Japanese flag that looks like "her home flag that also was a flaming sun on a clear field" (WOS 93). With that gesture she lays to rest the physical dominance of "actual" men, like Stephen and Thomas, and instead "re"turns to "mythic" man, *Sun*. At this point *Sun* loses its brutal glimmer; instead, it was "shining, crystal and sweet the day they buried the baby" (WOS 103).

"Discovering that the qualities society has defined as male--security and independence--are hers also, she achieves the treasure of wholeness and autonomy."[12] Ephanie learns to trust the Native American ways again. Instead of saying, "Bless me father for I have sinned," she now lets her fingers touch her thumbs, blessing one another, dedicating her gifts to the "sun," while pronouncing, "Bless me, Naiya Iyatiku, for I have been wronged" (WOS 153).

> She raised up in hope. Rose each dawn to watch eastward, make an offering of golden corn meal to the dawn. She held it to the sun. She gave it to the wind. . . . Ephanies's true name [was] Yellow Corn Woman (WOS 173).

Either as mediator between *Ts'its'tsi'nako* and her sister-goddesses or as an aspect of *Uretsete*, stands *Iyatiku*, the *Corn Mother*, who is of great importance in Pueblo ceremonies. Tyler states that "Iyatiku remains beneath in the four-chambered underworld, from which she first passes on information at the time of the Emergence." Later, he continues, "she receives the dead back again when they return to her realm." Her representation in Keres society is Iarriko, a perfect ear of corn, with each kernel in place right down to the tip. *Iyatiku* is thus the embodiment of "life-giving power as embodied in a fetish which is a part of herself."[13]

Among the Keres, yellow "is the color for women [and] it is the color ascribed to the Northwest." Allen continues in The Sacred Hoop: "Keres women paint their faces yellow on certain ceremonial occasions and are so painted at death so that the guardian at the gate of the spirit world, Naiya Iyatiku (Mother Corn Woman), will recognize that the newly arrived person is a woman."[14] Having moved to Oregon, the Northwest, and having found an identity as *Yellow Corn Woman*, her own clan mother and the Keres goddess responsible for the creation of women, "knowledge grew within her like the sun . . ." (WOS 179). It is only in keeping with the mythological symbolism that *Spider Woman*, "grandmother of the sun,"[15] enters the picture:

> What Grandmother Spider had taught, had left them to study in the full measure of their lives. At Guadalupe, recognizing the nature of her silent instruction, they called her Thinking Woman. She who is thinking. She who is waiting. For them to understand, to come in their hearts and minds to peace. The only possible hope (WOS 189).

Years later, when Ephanie returns to San Francisco, her older children are with her parents much of the time and the surviving twin, Tsali, lives with Thomas whom she divorced in the meantime. Ephanie spends much of her time alone, communicating mostly with Teresa, reading and studying. Freed from the responsibilities towards her children, Ephanie concentrates solely on her past experiences. By consciously trying to remember nearly forgotten incidents, Ephanie starts reliving her past and partly uncovers the events that led her to live a life marked by a series of personal devastations. Since at this point she is incapable of handling the emotional distress that accompanies her revelations, she attempt suicide and again falls "several feet to the waiting floor" (WOS 164). This time, however, she finds within herself a fierce determination to live. Looking at a spider who had watched her fall, "sitting unconcerned like spiders do [and] approving of her,"[16] Ephanie is finally able to say: "'Thanks, Grandmother. I think I'm going to be all right'" (WOS 164). *Spider Woman* thus provides spiritual affirmation amid Ephanie's defeatism.

Having finally learned that myths "are not sown like gardens [but] inherited from the past,"[17] Ephanie, in a desperate attempt to find her identity, reaches back to her own Pueblo mythologies and encounters *Spider Woman*. She realizes that the mythic designs of *Spider Woman*, the secular aspect of *Thought Woman*, creator-goddess of the Pueblos, provide one possible avenue out of the despair she currently experiences. She finds solace in the mythic figure of *Ts'its'tsi'nako*, "the feminine form for thought or reason,"[18] a powerful, dynamic entity who contains all life possibilities within herself. Ephanie finally uncovers "the source of her despair and isolation and is drawn into the spiritual life of the women of her people."[19] She regains parts of her former self-assurance by remembering the origin myth she had heard many years ago and by identifying with some aspects of *Ts'its'tsi'nako*'s creative scheme.

Although slight differences exist in each Pueblo, Keres mythology basically adheres to the following version of creation: in the beginning existed *Ts'its'tsi'nako*, "the overarching divinity of the Keres,"[20] along with her secular aspect, *Spider Woman*, or *Spider Grandmother*, and her dormant sisters. And since she can cause things to happen merely by thinking of them, *Ts'its'tsi'nako* thinks creation and sings her two sisters into life. In Keres theology creation does not take place through copulation. Rather, *Ts'its'tsi'nako*'s ideas are immediately put into thought turned into action. All her thoughts are thus realized, affirming the creative power of the word.

Ts'its'tsi'nako nursed the two sisters and taught them their language. She gave them each a basket of seeds and little images of all the kinds of animals that would eventually exist in the world. The two sisters created a badger and told him to make a hole in the crust to provide them with the opportunity to escape the darkness of the lower world. *Ts'its'tsi'nako* gave them instructions on what to do once they emerged and taught them the prayers and the creation song. Like Ephanie at the beginning of her "emergence" from the darkness of her torn psyche, the two sisters prayed to *Sun* as they had been taught and sang the creation song after reaching the earth. Soon *Naotsete* became pregnant and gave birth to twin boys. However, only one of the boys stayed with her; the other left with her younger sister, *Uretsete*.[21]

An aspect especially encouraging to Ephanie is the fact that *Ts'its'tsi'nako* did not restrict the process of creation to herself alone.[22] Realizing that she is endowed with the ability to 'think' and 'create', Ephanie finds a new affirmation of life within herself. By cutting the rope and evading her physical death, Ephanie simultaneously cuts the rope that had emotionally and psychologically tied up her true inner self. Through the life-giving myth of *Spider Woman* she has finally freed herself from the stifling bondages that had prevented her emotional maturity:

> In the third stage, the hero either literally or symbolically journeys to her ancestral home in search of her father, and discovers instead that it is her mother with whom she seeks to be rejoined. In this stage, a rescue figure aids the hero in freeing herself from the myth of female inferiority and in identifying a viable female tradition.[23]

Only after her innermost feelings surface again is she able to relive that most devastating experience of her childhood days. She remembers that Stephen had told her to jump from the tree, making her believe she was "an appleblossom, floating gently to the ground" (WOS 201). After Ephanie has reentered the mythical framework of her heritage and thereby achieved, at least in part, the psychic and spiritual integration of her being, not the Christian view of that initial fall dominates her feelings and thoughts, but the old Seneca myth of *Sky Woman*.

Sky Woman was told by her father to marry a man in a land far away. This man turned out to be a magician and sorcerer. In order to see if she was a fitting wife for him, he subjected her to a series of brutal and dangerous tests. She passed all of them since she herself has great psychic abilities. When he fell ill, his advisors told him to kill his wife, insinuating that she was the source of all his problems. Uprooting the "Tree of Light" in front of his home, he made her look into the abyss, trying to convince her to jump:

> "Jump?" She asked, looking down through the opening, trying to calculate the distance. "But it is very far."
> "Someone of your courage could do it," he said. "You could jump. Become the wind or a petal from this tree," he indicated the tree lying fallen next to them. "A petal could fall, gently, on the wind it would be carried. You could be a petal in the wind. You could be a butterfly, a downgliding brightbird [sic]" (WOS 194).

Being a dutiful wife she indeed jumped. While falling into the blue void she is caught by birds and rescued by waterfowl which gave their own lives in order to save her. Placed firmly on the back of "Grandmother Turtle," *Sky Woman* became the first human in a new world.[24] Having been impregnated by the "Tree of Light," she gave birth to a daughter who later bore twin boys.[25]

In Ephanie's memories the apple-tree of the Christian creation story gives way to the "Tree of Light" of the Seneca origin myth. Thus Ephanie no longer compares herself to Eve who, in Ephanie's opinion, had plunged all of humanity into sin forever. Instead, Ephanie now identifies with *Sky Woman* who created a new world and became the Mother of all. Ephanie abandons the thought that the animal and plant kingdoms (in form of the snake and the apple-tree) aided in the seduction of mankind. She subscribes instead to the notion of the Seneca myth that both the tree which impregnated *Sky Woman*, and various animals which carry her down safely, function as co-creators.

"A Lot Changed After She Fell," the chapter following "The Woman Who Fell From the Sky," suggests a continuation of *Sky Woman*'s endeavors. However, the chapter turns out to be a combination of Ephanie's fall from the apple tree and reflections of *Sky Woman*'s experiences. Thus, Ephanie's contemporary 'fall' from the tree is identified with *Sky Woman*'s mythical 'fall' from the sky. Ephanie now understands that what had "happened in time immemorial . . . happened now. Only the names were different" (WOS 191). Like Abel, Tayo, and Set before her, she understands that the hoop of existence forms a continuous circle, connecting through time and space events and myths, people and gods.

Ephanie finally realizes that the mythological tale of *Sky Woman*'s fall represents an alternative world view of woman stronger than man, of woman who arouses man's fear and jealousy, of woman "who fell beneath the shining boughs of the tree almost forever," but not quite. In her falling, *Sky Woman* entered "a new world and upon it planted her seed." It is she "who gave the sun and moon their light. Who from death made life. Who knew nothing was ever ended. Who just went on." Ephanie now realizes that everything is related, that falling into the void just means that a door is closing on one world and opening up on another. For Ephanie the Seneca story not only provides the foundation for an ethnic identity, but serves also as a means of reevaluating and developing her female authenticity. Towards the end of her long and painful journey, *Sun*, in accord with Ephanie's newly won insights, finally becomes a "clock, a calendar, like her body." Ephanie has at last reached the place where full integration is possible. "After she fell the sun went out" (WOS 203). Now it has begun to shine again.

At the end of her self-finding process, Ephanie understands, like Grey understood much earlier and without the painful emotional fragmentation that accompanies Ephanie's development, how her life parallels the life of the mythological women of "time immemorial." Through the empowering myth recounting *Spider Woman*'s creative design, Ephanie discovers the existence of an alternative world view in southwestern belief system. This leads her to the Seneca story of *Sky Woman* which enables her to unmask the sexist ideology that had stifled both her development as a woman as well as her emotional and spiritual growth. Ephanie is now able to wholeheartedly accept the novel's motto: "In the beginning was the Spider. She divided the world. She made it. Thinking thus she made the world. . . . There were no others then but the Spider who sang" (WOS 1). The Native American conception of woman--as creator not victim--acts as a powerful counterpart to Ephanie's former experiences.

Ephanie's search for psychic unity leads her back to the ritual awareness of her Keres people. Ephanie learns to understand how her life and the lives of other women parallel the lives of the goddess-figures in tribal narratives. As she understands this and as she lives out the implications of that understanding, she is able to accept both her place within the ritual tradition of her people and her responsibility to continue it. Her initial difficulty which she shares with Abel, Tayo, and Set, is realizing the importance of the mythic structure, not only as legends to pass on, but as viable traditions to continue.

Although Allen promises to write down the words *Spider Grandmother* thinks, thus adding an all-encompassing quality to her narration she, unlike Silko, takes the mythic context to comment on her protagonist's very personal despair. Ephanie's destiny has no immediate healing effect on her tribal community. This in itself would not constitute a problem--if it weren't for the author's promise to follow the Pueblo storytelling tradition. The individuality Ephanie proclaims and celebrates goes contrary to both her heritage and the author's claim. *Grandmother Spider* relates stories of an everlasting importance to her people; yet, Allen's concern is centered solely on her protagonist's thoughts and actions.

V. Conclusion

The protagonists' disequilibrium and their subsequent journey towards psychic balance are two of the most important aspects of House Made of Dawn, The Ancient Child, Ceremony, and The Woman Who Owned the Shadows. In many respects, Tayo, Set, Abel, and Ephanie are alike. In the beginning, none of these protagonists has a clear sense of belonging to either a people, a tradition, or a culture. The protagonists are physically and emotionally alienated from their native heritage either through their half-breed status and/or through their complete adoption of "white" ways. Yet, as each author reveals the reasons for his or her protagonist's alienation, he or she also presents another, more significant literary theme: that of the power and importance of not just the feminine principle but, as Antell calls it, "the mythic feminine principle." Abel, Set, Tayo, and Ephanie must knowingly participate in the rituals of "time immemorial" in order to realize the feminine principle upon which their own integration is based and through which they will be united with their native heritage. The four novelists, though different in style and execution, provide their protagonists with the possibility to return to tribal traditions as a way out of despair and uprootedness.

In Momaday's House Made of Dawn, the woman-figure seems to be a sideline character only. At first glance, the significance of her presence in the novel seems to be questionable. Only familiarity with *First Woman*, the Navajo deity of the origin story, turns Angela from a distant onlooker to an involved participant and a shaping force in Abel's life. Like her mythic prototype merely a rough draft of her potential, Angela nevertheless helps bring Abel into contact with the legends of his people, and thus with the traditional ways that create the emotional stability necessary to heal his wounded psyche.

In The Ancient Child, Momaday builds and elaborates on the myth of Mountain Chant, which also serves as an important symbolic framing device in House Made of Dawn. The further exploration of the Mountain Chant coincides with the added mythic significance of the female character. Although the novel centers on the spiritual improvement of the male protagonist, the woman-figure (unlike in House Made of Dawn) occupies a place in the novel's immediate foreground. Grey, as *Changing Woman* an evolved version of Angela's *First Woman*, is in tune with spiritual values and possesses all the physical and psychological characteristics attributed to her Navajo goddess prototype. In her function as shaman and medicine-woman, Grey is not only thoroughly aware of her role in Set's spiritual development, but indeed initiates, shapes, and furthers his mythic reintegration, and consequently, his self-finding process.

Not just one, but a whole cast of mythic female characters enables Tayo, the protagonist of Silko's Ceremony, to achieve psychic unity with his tribal heritage. The symbolic associations thread through the entire story like a spider's web and interconnect the mythic female figures which ultimately ensure Tayo's successful completion of the ceremony. With the help of Ts'eh, the contemporary aspect of *Yellow Woman*, Tayo becomes reintuned to his native heritage. Unlike Abel and Set, Tayo, a rather passive protagonist, does not strive towards heroic deeds or identification with powerful animal spirits; rather, for himself as well as for the other members of his tribe he desires a simple reemergence into the spiritual life of native tradition. As opposed to Momaday's novels, the predominant issue in Ceremony is not solely the well-being of the individual protagonist, but the general good of the entire tribe.

Ephanie, the central character in The Woman Who Owned the Shadows, differs from the previous protagonists not only in that she is female. Unlike the others, she does not have a guiding force in her life, providing her with the spiritual essentials and aiding her on her way to emotional balance. Instead, she has to rely on her own abilities and insights in order to heal her fragmented and disturbed self. Ephanie is a person at once deeply divided and strongly yearning for unity; she is both protagonist and feminine principle, down-to-earth woman and mythic archetype. Whereas all male protagonists enter the realm of Native American tradition through a female mythic archetype embodied in "real" women, Ephanie, being the "real" woman herself, establishes a more direct and undiluted connection to her mythic prototype, *Spider Woman.* Whereas Momaday and Silko address the power and significance of women through the characters of alienated men, Allen chose an estranged female protagonist to first reject and ultimately rediscover and identify with the goddess-figures of her people's myths.

After completion of the ritual which connects them to the mythic tradition, the novels' protagonists are eventually restored to spiritual harmony. Each protagonist needs to recognize that it is the women's identification with the creator-goddesses of the origin stories that enables him or her to fuse with their mythic heritage. Abel, Tayo, Set, and Ephanie finally acknowledge that their individual experience is not isolated but is part of a coherent and timeless whole, providing them with the means of personal empowerment and giving shape and direction to their lives.

True to his philosophy of the "sacredness of the word" and his rootedness in the individualistic tradition of Navajo art, Momaday's novels feature the concepts of both the creative power of words and the importance of identity. The protagonists' individual attainment of well-being is of paramount significance, not the tribes' overall and all-inclusive achievement of healthiness (both, Abel and Set run/go off by themselves at the end of their respective ordeals). Momaday employs themes and structures derived from oral accounts; yet the structural complexity and the thematic ambiguity in his works clearly disclose an individual "creator," not one simply re-telling traditional tales and teaching ancient values. Whereas the author of House Made of Dawn succeeds in creating a story rich in mythic symbolism and supernatural action, Momaday's concern with the development of his fictional characters--his "private products"--is overbearingly present and buries many larger mythic issues in The Ancient Child. The emphasis on the protagonist and his unique and singular search for identity and selfhood not only represents a distinctly "Navajo" way of artistic creation, but also closely resembles traditional Euro-American literature. His latest novel might be more accessible, but not necessarily more captivating or rewarding to readers used to western works.

By attributing their works to "Grandmother Spider," Allen and Silko, on the other hand, manage to carve out a niche for themselves within the Pueblo storyteller-tradition, a tradition which de-emphasizes both the significance of the author and the singularity of the protagonists and their actions. Especially Silko clearly perceives herself as conveyor, not originator, of her narrative; hence both tale and teller--like in traditional oral accounts--are embedded in a mythic framework. By observing Pueblo traditionalism more strictly and by exclusively focusing on Native American well-being, Silko emphasizes the function of her novel: the bringing together of either a native audience familiar with the traditional stories, or an audience willing to delve into native traditions and study the related symbolism. By excluding an unwilling or uninterested audience, Ceremony provides an example of Native American self-determination and self-confidence. Whereas Silko consistently abides by her traditional storyteller function throughout her narrative, Allen, like Momaday in The Ancient Child, chooses a mythic structure to support a seemingly autobiographic content. Through the authors' greater identification with and concern for their protagonists, these lose some of the eternal and mythic qualities indispensable for their archetypal role.

By readdressing their own mythic traditions, Allen, Momaday, and Silko, are able to counteract colonization and genocide. Rather than constructing violent or assimilationist solutions to their protagonists' alienation and sense of isolation, all three novelists develop plots which take the form of ancient mythic rituals, emphasizing integration rather than fragmentation. Their protagonists' aspirations towards healthiness in a mythic tribal context reflect Native America's persistent refusal to let go of tribal identity and to assimilate to western philosophical or literary concepts. By placing the solutions to their protagonists' contemporary despair in "time immemorial"--thus reconnecting in a circular mode to their tribal myths--Allen, Momaday, and Silko celebrate Native America's "sacred hoop" and simultaneously reject the concept of linear time and process.

By juxtaposing their contemporary characters with corresponding figures from the realm of mythology, the authors have succeeded in creating works that confirm the present-day viability of myths. Powerful symbols from the realm of mythology serve to comment on the events and characters of both mythic and contemporary times. Through this re-awakening of deeply buried archetypes from the origin myths of southwestern tribes, Allen, Momaday, and Silko address both the significance of tribal traditions and myths in general, and the continued and lasting importance of creator-goddesses in particular. Having resided in the collective memory of the people, the female archetypes are resurfacing once again to reclaim their due place in the lives of the Native American people.

ENDNOTES

1. James Welch, "Snow Country Weavers," South Dakota Review 28.

2. David Harvey, address, Closing General Sess., Deutsche Gesellschaft für Amerikastudien, Berlin, 12 June 1992.

3. Gregory S. Jay, "The End of 'American' Literature: Toward a Multicultural Practice," College English 266.

4. Paul Lauter, "The Literatures of America: A Comparative Discipline," Redefining American Literary History 22-23.

I. Introduction

1. Comp. "Wo hört die Mythologie auf, und wo fängt die Geschichte an?" Claude Lévi-Strauss, Mythos und Bedeutung 50.
I have either placed my translations (within apostrophes) into the text or translated all quotations under the corresponding endnote number.

2. Kenneth Lincoln, Native American Renaissance 13-14.

3. John Epes Brown, The Spiritual Legacy 2.

4. Northrop Frye, Myth and Metaphor: Selected Essays, 1974-1988 8.

5. "Wirklichkeitsrang bedeutet nicht den empirischen Nachweis; an seine Stelle kann Selbstverständlichkeit, Vertrautheit, archaische Weltzugehörigkeit treten." Hans Blumenberg, Arbeit am Mythos 78.

6. Mythen sind "Geschichten von hochgradiger Beständigkeit ihres narrativen Kerns und ebenso ausgeprägter marginaler Variationsfähigkeit." Mythen, behauptet er, "sind daher nicht so etwas wie »heilige« Texte, an denen jedes Jota unberührbar ist." Blumenberg 40.

7. Charlotte J. Frisbie, Southwestern Indian Ritual Drama 8.

8. "Der Grundmythos ist nicht das Vorgegebene, sondern das am Ende sichtbar Bleibende. . . . "; Blumenberg 192. "Festigkeit gegenüber den Abnutzungsprozessen der Zeit"; Blumenberg 177.

9. Leslie Marmon Silko, "Language and Literature from a Pueblo Indian Perspective," English Literature: Opening Up the Canon 69. To explain this phenomenon mythologically, Blumenberg writes on page 152: "Gerade weil die Funktion des Mythos auf die Weltsicherheit des Menschen zentriert ist, ist der Komplex seiner Gestalten und Geschichten nicht anthropozentrisch." ('Since the function of myth focuses on the safety of mankind, the array of its characters and stories is not anthropocentric').

10. Paula Gunn Allen, The Sacred Hoop: Recovering the Feminine in American Indian Tradition 73-74.

11. Sam Gill, Native American Religious Action: A Performance Approach to Religion n.p.

12. David Bidney, "Myth, Symbolism, and Truth," Myth and Literature: Contemporary Theory and Practice 7. In accordance with the Native American usage of the word "symbol," the term will hereafter be employed to refer to a sign which unequivocally coincides with analogous aspects in mythology.

13. N. Scott Momaday, House Made of Dawn; hereafter cited as HMD.
Leslie Marmon Silko, Ceremony; hereafter cited as C.
Paula Gunn Allen, The Woman Who Owned the Shadows; hereafter cited as WOS.
N. Scott Momaday, The Ancient Child; hereafter cited as AC.
All citations will be included parenthetically in the text. For better reading, all quotations that are **not** followed by either parentheses or endnote numbers will automatically be included in the next mention of sources. In order to avoid confusion between mythic and fictional characters, the names of all mythic figures, human or non-human, will be in italics. In those parts of the dissertation that deal with mythology there might at times occur a rather sudden change of tense. This is due to the fact that some mythic events or supernatural orders are finished whereas comparable others are of an everlasting quality.

14. Allen, Sacred Hoop 241.

II. Historical Survey
i. the United States

1. Lincoln, Native American Renaissance 19.

2. This number is by far the highest estimate among scholars.

3. Allen, Sacred Hoop 189-190.

4. Allen, Sacred Hoop 3-4. Allen describes gynocracies as "woman-centered tribal societies" which feature "matrilocality, matrifocality, matrilinearity, maternal control of household goods and resources" as the primary social order. She further asserts that male dominance may have "characterized a number of tribes, but it was by no means as universal (or even as preponderant) as colonialist propaganda has led us to believe" (Sacred Hoop 32).

5. Allen, Sacred Hoop 263.

6. Peggy Reeves Sanday, Female Power and Male Dominance: On the Origins of Sexual Inequality 25, 27.

7. Peter Farb, Man's Rise to Civilization: The Cultural Ascent of the Indians of North America 92. Comp. also Reeves Sanday 28. Furthermore, archaeological excavations of pre-Iroquoian village sites show that they were unfortified, suggesting that any possible emphasis on warfare definitely lacked major economic motivation. In these sites, horticulture clearly took precedence over fishing and hunting, both considered male activities. Houses contained several hearths and appeared to be early prototypes of the longhouse providing shelter for families that were related through the female line. One can infer from this evidence that the village was the primary sociopolitical unit and that matrifocality superseded patrifocality (comp. Reeves Sanday 117-118).

8. John P. Brown, Old Frontiers 20. Cited in Carolyn Foreman, Indian Women Chiefs 7. The Iroquoian tribes had another custom that confirms the significance of women. They set the penalty for killing a woman at double that for killing a man. This regulation was in force at least among the Susquehanna, the Hurons, and the Iroquois; but given the significance women held, and given that in killing a woman one killed the children she might have born, the practice of doubling the penalty was probably common (comp. Allen, Sacred Hoop 32).

9. Comp. Allen, Sacred Hoop 37. In an effort to escape removal, according to Allen, the Cherokee "drafted a constitution in the early 1800s that disenfranchised women and blacks. Modeled after the Constitution of the United States, whose favor they were attempting to curry, and in conjunction with Christian sympathizers to the Cherokee cause, the new Cherokee constitution relegated women to the position of chattel" (Allen, Sacred Hoop 37).

10. Charles Woodard, ed., Ancestral Voice: Conversations with N. Scott Momaday 66.

11. Allen, Sacred Hoop 36.

12. Allen, Sacred Hoop 41-42.

13. D'Arcy McNickle 72.

14. Farb 242. Besides the deaths resulting from removals or intertribal wars, the greatest cause of death was disease. The west was swept by numerous diseases hitherto unknown to native tribes. Only a hundred Mandan out of a population of sixteen hundred survived a smallpox epidemic; the same epidemic, spreading westward, reduced the total number of Blackfoot by about half. The majority of the Kiowa and Comanche tribes were victims of cholera.

15. Innumerable at the beginning of the eighteenth century, the buffalo was the life-support of the Plains tribes. With the buffalo, whose significance for the tribes cannot be overemphasized, a culture died. Lame Deer affirms the importance of the buffalo in Lame Deer: Seeker of Visions:

> The buffalo gave us everything we needed. Without it we were nothing. Our tipis were made of his skin. His hide was our bed, our blanket, our winter coat. It was our drum, throbbing through the night, alive, holy. Out of his skin we made our water bags. His flesh strengthened us, became flesh of our flesh. Not the smallest part of it was wasted. His stomach, a red-hot stone dropped into it, became our soup kettle. His horns were our spoons, the bones our knives, our women's awls and needles. Out of his sinews we made our bowstrings and thread. His ribs were fashioned into sleds for our children, his hoofs became rattles. His mighty skull, with the pipe leaning against it, was our sacred altar. The name of the greatest of all Sioux was Tatanka Iyotake - Sitting Bull. When you killed off the buffalo, you also killed the Indian - the real, natural, 'wild' Indian.

16. Lame Deer, Siouan medicine man, gives a moving account of his experiences at the white man's school:

> I went to the day school on the Rosebud Reservation, twelve miles south of Norris, South Dakota. The Government teachers were all third-grade teachers. They taught up to this grade and that was the highest. I stayed in that goddam [sic] third grade for six years. There weren't any other. The Indian people of my generation will tell you that it was the same at the other schools all over the reservations. Year after year the same grade over again. If we ran away the police would bring us back. It didn't matter anyway. In all those years at the day school they never taught me to speak English or to write and read. I learned these things only many years later, in saloons, in the army or in jail. John (Fire) Lame Deer, and Richard Erdoes, Lame Deer: Seeker of Visions 24.

17. Black Elk, Black Elk Speaks. Being the Life Story of a Holy Man of the Oglala Sioux 79. Comp. also Lincoln, Native American Renaissance 94.

18. Black Elk Speaks 134.

19. Farb 243.

20. Allen, Sacred Hoop 266.

21. Tom Bahti, Southwestern Indian Ceremonials 4.

22. Woodard 9.

23. ". . . religiöse Überzeugungen galten und gelten dem Indianer als eine ganz persönliche Erfahrung, über die man nicht diskutiert oder gar streitet. Oft ließen sich Indianer aus Höflichkeit taufen, um die drängenden Missionare nicht zu beleidigen." N. Scott Momaday, Der Weg zum Regenberg, trans. Peter Baum, 97.

24. Comp. Marla N. Powers, Oglala Women: Myth, Ritual and Reality 193.

25. Lincoln, Native American Renaissance 20-21; comp. also pp. 184-187. According to Lincoln the definition of "American Indian" is minimally a quarter blood and tribal membership. California has the highest American Indian population today, officially counted in the 1980 census at 201,311. Oklahoma ranks second with 169,000 American Indians.

26. Vine Deloria, Jr., God is Red 254, 50.

27. N. Scott Momaday, The Names. A Memoir 74-75.

28. Judith A. Antell, "Momaday, Welch and Silko: Expressing the Feminine Principle Through Male Alienation," American Indian Quarterly 214.

29. Allen, Sacred Hoop 42.

ii. the southwest

1. For a detailed analysis of southwestern prehistory, see: Alfonso Ortiz, ed., New Perspectives on the Pueblos, and Richard Erdoes, The Rain Dance People: The Pueblo Indians, their Past and Present.

2. Tiwa is spoken in the Taos, Picuris, Sandia and Isleta Pueblos. Tewa is spoken in the San Juan, Santa Clara, San Ildefonso, Nambe, Tesuque and Pojoaque Pueblos. Towa is spoken only by the Jemez. The Keresan language is spoken by the Acoma, Cochiti, Laguna, San Felipe, Santa Ana, Santo Domingo, and Zia Pueblos. The Zuni language is spoken by the Zunis only. Anthropologists have classified the Pueblos as "eastern" and "western" according to certain considerations of social and cultural differences. Generally, the Pueblos of Hopi, Zuni, Laguna, and Acoma have been placed in the western Pueblo division. The Keresan Pueblos as well as the Tanoan Pueblos and Jemez are designated as eastern, or Rio Grande Pueblos. They are located in six counties of present-day New Mexico. Comp. Joe S. Sando, The Pueblo Indians 2-4.

3. Comp. Edward P. Dozier, The Pueblo Indians of North America 137-141.

4. According to his research on a Navajo archaeological site, David Aberle asserts that the Navajo arrived in the Southwest some time prior to 1541. David Aberle, "Some Sources of Flexibility in Navaho Social Organizations," Southwestern Journal of Anthropology 1-8. Other historians, however, still

proclaim the rather uncertain history of the Navajo in preliterate times. See Bertha Dutton, Navahos and Apaches. The Athabascan Peoples 1-2.

5. Elsie Clews Parsons, Kiowa Tales xiii. For a description of further parallels with other tribes, see pages xiii-xxi. See also: Richard I. Ford, Albert H. Schroeder, and Stewart L. Peckham, "Three Perspectives on Puebloan Prehistory," New Perspectives on the Pueblos 32-34.

6. James J. Hester, Navajo Migrations and Acculturation 91.

7. Gladys A. Reichard, Navaho Religion: A Study of Symbolism 171; and Social Life of the Navajo Indians 52.

8. Tom Bahti, Southwestern Indian Tribes 4.

9. Hamilton A. Tyler, Pueblo Gods and Myths 159,260.

10. Dozier 70.

11. Sacred Hoop 45.

12. Charles W. Hacketts, Revolt of the Pueblo Indians of New Mexico cvi.

13. Dutton 8. Paul G. Zolbrod writes that the Navajos "were slower than the Pueblos to resist the Spaniards and much more restrained in their collective decision to carry on a policy of reprisal. The Navajos . . . appear to have maintained an implicit preference to be left alone. . . ." (Dine bahane': The Navajo Creation Story 414; hereafter cited parenthetically in the text as Dinė. There is evidence that the image of the Athabascan people needs reconsideration. Rather than being "warlike," new historical research deems it possible that they were more inclined to trade with the sedentary Pueblos, who relied on them for hides to be used for blankets and clothing. The Navajos seem to have cultivated their aggressive ways only as a reaction to Spanish oppression and atrocities (Dinė 413-414).

14. Bahti, Southwestern Indian Tribes 5.

15. Dutton 11.

16. Warren A. Beck, New Mexico: A History of Four Centuries 189.

17. Lame Deer 205.

18. Edward H. Spicer, Cycles of Conquest: The Impact of Spain, Mexico, and the United States on the Indians of the Southwest, 1533-1960 538.

III. Philosophical/Mythological Survey
i. philosophy

1. Brown, Spiritual Legacy ix.

2. Dozier 151.

3. 'Magical thinking does not allow for a fundamental differentiation between things and persons, substances containing and substances not containing a soul, between objects which can be manipulated, and agents capable of actions and oral discourse'. Jürgen Habermas, "Die Verschlingung von Mythos und Aufklärung: Bemerkungen zur *Dialektik der Aufklärung* - nach einer erneuten Lektüre," Mythos und Moderne: Begriff und Bild einer Rekonstruktion 414. In the creation myths of the Plains tribes, for example, animals were created before human beings. Therefore, both in their proximity to *Wakan-Tanka* and in their function as intermediaries between human beings and the supernatural(s) they demand respect and veneration. This explains not only why religious devotions may be directed to the deity through the animals, but it also helps us understand why contact with the *Great Spirit* comes to American Indians almost exclusively through visions involving animals (comp. Brown, Spiritual Legacy 38-40). In all the Pueblos, as Dozier points out, coyote, eagle, bear, and lion are accorded special attention since all are regarded in a ritual context as essentially human. Especially the bear whose forelegs are made into a kind of glove used in curing rituals possesses great healing powers as the special curing companion of the medicine man (comp. Dozier 160).

4. "Concepts of time that may be termed linear tend to be of relatively recent origin. It emerged with certain Judaic perspectives, became pervasive in the Western world with the beginnings of the European Renaissance, and was intensified through the rapidly changing ideologies of the Reformation. Obviously a concomitant of the progressive detraditionalization of the Western world, this process has proliferated throughout other once traditional worlds with great rapidity. . . . Linear time and process is not just a neutral quantitative scale of measurement, but is inseparable from the value orientations that give rise to it in the first place. There is the inevitable assumption that that which came earlier on this scale is somehow inferior to the more recent, or to that in the future toward which we are moving. Modern people have here found justification for maintaining their assumed inherent, even genetic, superiority over all those other populations of ancient origin who have not yet entered into this new vision of progressive time" (Brown, Spiritual Legacy 116-117). For further readings on the political and social implications of a predominantly linear concept of time consult Brown, Spiritual Legacy 117-121.

5. Black Elk Speaks 194-196. Describing myths in general, Blumenberg calls their cyclical nature "Grundriß des Weltvertrauens," the 'ground-plan of utter confidence' (97).

6. Jamake Highwater, The Primal Mind: Vision and Reality in Indian America 169.

7. Vine Deloria, Jr., We Talk-You Listen. New Tribes-New Turfs 33.

8. Washington Matthews, trans., Navaho Legends 33.

9. A. M. Stephen, Hopi Journal 584; as quoted in Tyler, Pueblo Gods and Myths 125. The change in sex can oftentimes be traced from east to west. A Pueblo example shows that in more western located Pueblos *Ts'its'tsi'nako* has two sisters; in some Laguna accounts, however, her oldest sister is transformed into a "brother," a development which Boas attributes to the influence of Christianity. All of his Laguna informants, Boas points out, agreed that the white man has a father, not necessarily a mother. Comp. Franz Boas, Keresan Texts 221.

10. Allen, Sacred Hoop 41, 42.

11. Bidney 7.

12. Myth and Metaphor 7.

13. James Ruppert, "The Reader's Lesson in 'Ceremony,'" Arizona Quarterly 79.

14. N. Scott Momaday, "The Man Made of Words," Literature of the American Indians: Views and Interpretations 103.

15. Lame Deer 105.

16. Momaday, Man Made of Words 107.

17. Momaday, Man Made of Words 98-99.

18. The "first world," "fire," and "flood" are references to the creation myths of many southwestern tribes who share the belief in the emergence to their present land after a migration through several underground worlds filled with floods or fire. "Dawn," Schubnell writes, "marks the moment of emergence from the underworld, the beginning of tribal life, and the creation of tribal culture." Matthias Schubnell, N. Scott Momaday. The Cultural and Literary Background 135-136.

19. Brown, Spiritual Legacy 76.

ii. oral tradition

1. Momaday, Man Made of Words 103. LaVonne Brown Ruoff writes in "American Indian Literatures: A Guide to Anthologies, Texts, and Research": "When Columbus mistook the Bahamas for India, Native America north of Mexico contained more than three hundred cultural groups, each with different customs, social structures, and world views. These cultural groups spoke 250 separate languages plus many dialects, derived from seven basic language families. . . . Such diversity precluded the existence of a single American Indian culture of literature - a fact essential to understanding the complexity

of American Indian oral literatures." Studies in American Indian Literature: Critical Essays and Course Designs 282.

2. Joseph Epes Brown, See n.p.; as quoted in Highwater, The Primal Mind 90.

3. "selektive Leistung der Mündlichkeit"; Blumenberg 169; comp. Blumenberg 170: "Die mündliche Überlieferung begünstigt die Prägnanz ihrer Gehalte zu Lasten der historischen oder vermeintlich historischen Präzision."

4. Dennis Tedlock, "Pueblo Literature: Style and Verisimilitude," New Perspectives on the Pueblos 221.

5. Geary Hobson, The Remembered Earth: An Anthology of Native American Literature 170.

6. Lauter, 24.

7. Sacred Words 49.

8. Silko, Language and Literature 54.

9. Silko 110.

10. Paula Gunn Allen, "Special Problems in Teaching Leslie Marmon Silko's 'Ceremony'," American Indian Quarterly 383.

11. Bronislaw Malinowski, "Myth in Primitive Society," Magic, Science, Religion, and Other Essays 77. As quoted in Jarold Ramsey, Reading The Fire: Essays in the Traditional Indian Literature of the Far West 4.

12. Allen, Sacred Hoop 79-80.

13. Gill, Religious Action 25. Allen maintains that western fiction, in contrast, is based on nonsacred aesthetic and intellectual precepts such as the importance of the unities of time, place, and action. Furthermore, western literature is structured to create the illusion of change in the characters occurring over a period of time as a result of conflict and crisis. With the exception of Joyce, she writes, western novels are not ritual-based and the incorporation of elements drawn from ritual-based cultures are mere intellectual, aesthetic, or allusive borrowings (comp. Allen, Sacred Hoop 62-64; 70ff).

iii. reality and mythology

1. Gill, Religious Action 24. Since there exist variants in orthography due to the vast dialect diversity from town to town among the eastern and western Pueblos, the Hopi, and the Navajos, I have used Paula Gunn Allen's versions of all Pueblo names, including the Hopi (as displayed in The Sacred Hoop),

and Zolbrod's version of Navajo names (as displayed in Dinė). Less emphasis will be placed on Zunian mythology since the existence of some divinities has been questioned by a variety of scholars (comp. Tyler, Pueblo Gods and Myths 85). Also, available Zuni accounts of their divinities are rather abstract in nature and exhibit "little historical shape" (Pueblo Gods and Myths 89; 94). Furthermore, many Zunian myths exhibit "Yuman rather than Pueblo" traits (Pueblo Gods and Myths 88).

2. Silko, Language and Literature 57.

3. "It is no oversimplification to assert that in Navajo society a genuinely poetic recitation must accompany the building of a new house, the treatment of a broken leg or of insomnia, the resolution of a dispute, the unwanted intrusion of a stranger, or the announcement of a pregnancy. Without the appropriate performance, in fact, certain everyday tasks cannot be accomplished" (Dinė 25).

4. Charlotte J. Frisbie, Navajo Medicine Bundles or **Jish**: Acquisition, Transmission, and Disposition in the Past and Present 1.

5. Leland C. Wyman, The Mountainway of the Navajo 61.

6. Allen, Sacred Hoop 43-44.

7. As has been noted above, influential historians and ethnologists agree that the existence of any male creators in native religion is the direct result of contact with Christian missionaries and the subsequent influx of patriarchal societies. Comp. Boas, Keresan Texts 221-222, and Mc Nickle 50.

8. "The neighboring Yurok, Karok, and Hupa of northwestern California share a single body of myth, while speaking totally unrelated languages. Both the Hupa and the distant Navajo speak Athabascan languages, yet their mythologies have nothing significant in common." Bierhorst, The Mythology of North America 16.

9. Brown, Spiritual Legacy 20.

10. Karl W. Luckert, A Navajo Holyway Healing Ceremonial 3, 5. Paul G. Zolbrod, "When Artifacts Speak, What Can They Tell Us?" Recovering the Word: Essays on Native American Literature 37. According to Zolbrod the Navajo creation story is the most comprehensive American Indian emergence myth that has found its way into printed English. The Navajos appear to have acquired their ideas about emergence from the Anasazi by way of the Pueblos. Although the emergence story belonged to the Pueblos before the Navajo received it, the available Navajo versions are the most comprehensive. Furthermore, as Zolbrod explains, Pueblo languages greatly vary from one community to the next that linguistic groups are too small to permit generalization. The Navajos, on the other hand, speak "a fairly uniform

language" and are also "less unwilling to share their traditions with outsiders than the more conservative Pueblo tribes . . ." (Dinė 4).

11. Comp. Blumenberg 116.

12. Tyler, Pueblo Gods and Myths 103, 107-108.

13. Reichard writes in Navaho Religion 125: "The nearest Navaho approach to the concept of sin is 'being out of order, lacking control,' a definition that involves rationalization, not salving a bad conscience; confession of error, not a feeling of guilt; laying on of hands, not a plea for forgiveness; propitiation, not expiation; identification with deity, not humiliation of the offender; and in the end, a sense of human achievement, not of subservience to divinity."

14. Clyde Kluckhohn and Dorothea Leighton, The Navajo 15.

15. The Navajo mythology consists of two major parts - the general origin myth, which includes the emergence from the underworlds, and the origin legends of the separate ceremonials that branch off from the origin myth at various points. The Navajo's mythology, writes Wyman, "is a unit composed of interlocking parts, filled with vivid word imagery, fine ritual poetry, keen humor, and great imaginative power" (Wyman, Mountainway 9).

16. Karl W. Luckert, The Navajo Hunter Tradition 133ff.

17. Karl W. Luckert, Coyoteway: A Navajo Holyway Healing Ceremonial 126. "In the beginning," Luckert continues, "all 'people' were able to exchange their appearances like clothes. When eventually mankind and many animals became fixed permanently in their present shapes, the gods remained in a state of prehuman flux" (Coyoteway 128).

18. Reichard, Navaho Religion 568, 569, 571, and 573.

19. Reichard, Navaho Religion 16. In the Navajo emergence narrative, *First Man* and *First Woman* traveled upward through four underworlds into the present Fifth World. In the Fourth World the two scouts who were sent out to scan the landscapes encountered "a strange race unlike any other." These were people who "cut their hair square in front. They were people who lived in houses in the ground. They were people who cultivated the soil so that things grew therein" (Dinė 46). Haile indicates that the origin of the Pueblos is "usually passed over in silence in Navajo legends and is accepted as an accomplished fact." Origin Legend of the Navaho Enemy Way 17.

20. Zolbrod, Artifacts 300.

21. Lawrence J. Evers, "Words and Place: A Reading of 'House Made of Dawn'" Western American Literature 299. Concerning the cloud pillars, Reichard writes that there are "four of whiteshell at the east, four of turquoise at the south, four of abalone at the west, four of redstone at the north"

(Navaho Religion 14). The inner mountains, Gobernador Knob and Herfano Mesa are the most important mountains inside Navajo land, especially in the origin story. Frisbie writes that due "to the existence of inner and boundary sacred mountains, variations occur in reference to the number of sacred mountains, with four or six being most common" (Navajo Medicine Bundles 431; endnote # 3).

22. Gill, Religious Action 18-19. "Long life" is the English translation of *sa'ah naaghâii*; "happiness" has been rendered as *bik'eh hózhó*. Haile maintains that these two are twin female deities, placed forever among the stars. Other opinions include the idea that *Asdzáá nádleehé*, *Changing Woman*, is the child of *Long Life Boy* and *Happiness Girl*, thus the child of two basic Navajo ideals. Comp. Fr. Berard Haile, Starlore Among the Navaho 384, 385. This theory would identify *sa'ah naaghâii* and *bik'eh hózhó* with *Altsé asdzáá* (*First Man*), and *Altsé hastiin* (*First Woman*), who are often considered the parents of *Asdzáá nádleehé*, *Changing Woman*.

23. *Changing Woman* sometimes has a sister, *Yoolgai asdzáá* (*White Shell Woman*); at other times, *Changing Woman* combines both characters and characteristics within herself. The discovery of *Changing Woman* and *White Shell Woman* is one of the great Navajo mysteries. Haile indicates that the answers to questions about the two goddesses remain concealed in esoteric knowledge carefully guarded by a small group of medicine men (Diné 382). In some variants of the Navajo creation myth *Changing Woman* has intercourse with both sunlight and water (see Diné 387 for a set of references to such texts), in which case she would be the mother of both *Monster-Slayer* and *Born-of-Water*. In other versions of the myth *Monster-Slayer* is *Changing Woman's* son whereas *White Shell Woman* gives birth to *Born-of-Water*. Despite all variations in the available mythical accounts, the two offspring, *Monster-Slayer* and *Born-of-Water*, are commonly regarded as twins. Notwithstanding the possibility of their different origin, *Sun* later on assumes the paternal role for both heroes (Diné 389). Reichard identifies the son of *White Shell Woman* as "the gentle, pacific, steady foil to the active, impulsive Monster Slayer." Further, she continues, "pairing is an illustration of a cultural compulsion" (Reichard, Navaho Religion xxiii; 248-249).

24. Frisbie, Navajo Medicine Bundles 2.

25. Gary Witherspoon, Language and Art in the Navajo Universe 202.

26. Bierhorst, The Mythology of North America 99. The myth of Blessingway is most intimately associated with the origin myth, being mostly concerned with the post-emergence events; thus Blessingway reveals the origin of many elements of Navajo culture.

IV. Mythological Women in Contemporary Literature
i. introductory remarks

1. Silko, Language and Literature 54.

2. John Bierhorst, ed., In the Trail of the Wind: American Indian Poems and Ritual Orations 4-5.

3. William Bevis, "American Indian Verse Translations," Literature of the American Indians: Essays and Interpretations 582, 585.

4. Allen, Sacred Hoop 108.

5. Paula Gunn Allen, "Bringing Home the Fact: Tradition and Continuity in the Imagination," Recovering the Word: Essays on Native American Literature 564.

6. Lincoln, for example, writes in Native American Renaissance 119: "A more insidious threat appears in the condescension of Angela Grace Martin St. John, a Beverly Hills matron who journeys to Jemez for the healing waters. Angela stays on to seduce the priest's woodcutter, Abel, [and] goes slumming religion and race to pursue 'the last reality' beyond all things seen and known." Frauke Zwillus' commentary constitutes a notable exception. She writes that "erst die leidenschaftliche sexuelle Affaire mit Abel verhilft ihr zu einem natürlichen Umgang mit Erotik und Körperlichkeit. Für Angela ist somit der Kontakt mit der indianischen Welt heilsam und führt zu einer inneren Wandlung." 'Only the passionate sexual affair with Abel helps her deal in a natural way with her sensuality. For Angela, the contact with the Native American world has not only been helpful, but has even initiated fundamental changes within her inner self'. Frauke Zwillus, Today's Talk in Yesterday's Voice 68.

ii. N. Scott Momaday/House Made of Dawn

1. Momaday was born in 1934 in Oklahoma. He spent his childhood on a Navajo reservation; in 1946 he and his parents moved to Jemez Pueblo. Momaday began publishing poetry in The New Mexico Quarterly (1959) as an undergraduate at the University of New Mexico. He received a Stanford doctorate in American literature in 1963, a Guggenheim Fellowship in 1966, the Pulitzer Prize for Fiction in 1969 (for House Made of Dawn), and in 1973 a professorship in English and comparative literature at his alma mater, Stanford University. In 1981 he joined the American Indian Studies faculty at the University of Arizona, along with Vine Deloria, Jr., and Leslie M. Silko. In 1989 he published his second novel, The Ancient Child.

2. N. Scott Momaday, interview, "Story Teller," The Journal of Ethnic Studies 120.

3. "The name *Yeibichai*," writes Bahti in Southwestern Indian Ceremonials 10, "is used for the Night Way because of the appearance of numerous *Yeis* (masked representations of supernatural beings which possess great powers)

during the last two nights of this nine-day ceremony." It is a dangerous ritual, for mistakes made by either the patient or singer during its performance can result in crippling, facial paralysis or a loss of sight or hearing. On the eighth night the Yeibichais conduct an initiation rite to introduce Navajo boys and girls to the secret of the masked gods. "The boys are blessed with sacred meal and then ceremonially whipped with yucca leaves by the masked figures. The girls are marked on the feet, hands, shoulders and head with ears of white and yellow corn wrapped in spruce twigs. Shortly afterwards the *Yeis* remove their masks so the children learn they are really ordinary human beings who only play the part of supernatural figures. *Hastseyalti*, the Talking God of the East, places his mask on each of the boys while *Hasttse-baad*, the female *Yei*, places hers on the girls so that each child may view the world through the eyes of the *Yeibichais*."

4. Carl H. Gorman, "Navajo Vision of Earth and Man," The Indian Historian 21. "House Made of Dawn" is the first line of the chant sung on the third day of the Night Chant. It is the first prayer of the third morning ritual; the third day is designated the Day of the West.

5. Reichard, Navaho Religion 328. Both, the Night Chant as well as the Mountain Chant are part of the larger subgroup of the Blessingway rites. There are six main groups of chants or song ceremonials although some have become obsolete through disuse. The Night Chant cures insanity and paralysis, the Mountain Chant is mainly concerned with the healing of nervousness and emotional instability.

6. John Bierhorst, ed., Four Masterworks of American Indian Literature: Quetzacoatl/The Ritual of Condolence/Cuceb/The Night Chant 282.

7. Whereas Zolbrod indicates that *Changing Woman* and *White Shell Woman* were "created" at the same time and are thus sisters, most accounts favor the version that *Changing Woman* created *White Shell Woman* and *Turquoise Woman* from the rubbings of her own skin. They would therefore be considered her daughters/sisters (Reichard, Navaho Religion 494-495). This version would place them into closer proximity to the Pueblo goddess *Ts'its'tsi'nako* who also created two female deities, *Naotsete* and *Uretsete*, considered her coequals. The protagonist of the Night Chant repeatedly identifies with *Changing Woman*'s son, *Monster-Slayer*: "The Slayer of the Alien Gods That now am I" (Bierhorst, Four Masterworks 303).

8. Reichard, Navaho Religion 152.

9. Brown, Spiritual Legacy 74.

10. Hamilton A. Tyler, Pueblo Animals and Myths 190-193.

11. Schubnell 108.

12. Reichard, Navaho Religion 5.

13. Allen, Sacred Hoop 87.

14. Reichard, Navaho Religion 437.

15. Reichard, Navaho Religion 63, 26.

16. Reichard, Navaho Religion 192.

17. Edith Swan, "Laguna Symbolic Geography and Silko's 'Ceremony'," American Indian Quarterly 240, 246.

18. Swan 239.

19. Wyman, Mountainway 149.

20. Swan 239.

21. Allen, Sacred Hoop 63.

22. Gill, Religious Action 97.

23. The animal Momaday mentions is a "bobcat or a fox" (HMD 52); however, as Tyler points out in Pueblo Animals and Myths, 121: "Gray Fox . . . in modern times stands in for . . . Mountain Lion."

24. Allen, Sacred Hoop 71.

25. Reichard, Navaho Religion 53.

26. Bierhorst, Four Masterworks 304.

27. Washington Matthews, "Navaho Myths, Prayers, and Songs With Texts and Translations," American Archaeology and Ethnology 29.

28. Reichard, Navaho Religion 624.

29. Reichard, Navaho Religion 195.

30. Matthew W. Stirling, Origin Myth of Acoma and Other Records 2. In the Navajo creation story, Badger was created in the Fourth World "when the sky touched the earth and the earth touched the sky." Just then, "at exactly the spot where the sky and the earth had met . . . *Nahashch'id* the Badger sprung out of the ground" (Dinė 56). Ever since the time of emergence, great healing powers have been attributed to ***Badger***. Another interesting myth mentions that he had the power to raise the dead. When witches had killed *Yellow Woman*, the Ka't'sinas sent for ***Badger*** to make her come to life again. After ***Badger*** had sung "for each direction," *Yellow Woman* started breathing. However, ***Badger*** said that she could only appear at night since her heart was hidden in "White House." *Yellow Woman*'s nightly appearances further

emphasize her close association with the moon (comp. Tyler, Pueblo Animals and Myths 29).

31. Schubnell 120.

32. Stirling 87.

33. Alfonso Ortiz, "Ritual Drama and the Pueblo World View," New Perspectives on the Pueblos 151.

34. Leland C. Wyman, "Navajo Ceremonial System," Handbook of North American Indians 536-537.

35. He is possibly modeled after Momaday's paternal grandfather, Mammedaty, who, "shrewd in matters of the world . . . was a peyote priest in his prime and a Christian in his last years" (Momaday, The Names 32).

36. Schubnell 129.

37. Tyler, Pueblo Animals and Myths 227-228.

38. Deloria, God is Red 180.

39. Reichard, Navaho Religion 187.

40. Schubnell 129.

41. Bierhorst, Four Masterworks 303.

42. Bierhorst, Four Masterworks 285.

43. Gill, Religious Action 96-97.

44. Evers 316-317. Zolbrod writes: "The central theme is the attainment of *hózhó*, a fairly untranslatable term which can only be approximated in English by combining words like *beauty, balance,* and *harmony*" (Diné 5). Furthermore, the Night Chant mentions "pollen" which according to Matthews' explanation brings peace, happiness, and prosperity. Washington Matthews, The Night Chant 42.

45. Allen, Sacred Hoop 117.

46. Like in Pueblo thought, the Navajo cosmology is physically encircled by the four sacred mountains of the cardinal directions. Blessingway rites, the backbone of Navajo religion, require a mountain soil bundle, containing pinches of soil from the summits of the sacred mountains. The Mountain Chant, however, deals with mountains in general. There exists a considerable degree of variation in the tales of different informants. These dissimilarities, as Wyman writes, "could result from such factors as geographical variants, peculiarities of a 'school' of singers, incomplete narration, deliberate

abbreviation, invention by the narrator, imperfect interpretation or translation, and intrinsic differences representative of different chantways." Leland C. Wyman, ed., Beautyway: A Navajo Ceremonial 23-24. Therefore, I have focused on the essential plot of the story which is agreed upon by most informants. Other versions mention the fact that the sisters had twelve brothers, all but two of whom were killed by the Pueblos. This, however, may only be a justification for the raid on Taos (comp. Beautyway 32). In some versions, *Older Sister*, the wife of *Bear Man*, "saw the first Mountain Chant" and was taken on a long journey by the *Holy People* to learn ritual lore (comp. Beautyway 31).
Enemyway, as opposed to Blessingway which emphasizes peace and harmony, is used to exorcise evil forces and counteract the effects of witchcraft. "The Mountainway myths," according to Wyman, "are remarkably uniform with regard to the Navajo group which instigates the war with the Pueblo Indians." The Beautyway myths agree, he maintains, "that the attack on the Pueblos is unprovoked [and] instigated frankly as a trophy hunt, a contest for warriors vying to win the two beautiful Navajo maidens as prizes for taking the scalps of the non-sunlight-struck Pueblo beings, rather than being reprisal for losses suffered in previous battles" (Wyman, Mountainway 130-131). In House Made of Dawn, the narrator seems to suggest that the Pueblo raid was the result of a Pueblo attack on the Navajo: "Grandson, it was here, here at Kin tqel that they killed two of the cave people" (HMD 170).

47. Wyman, Mountainway 18ff.

48. Reichard, Navaho Religion 322.

49. Allen, Critical Essays 176-177.

50. Momaday, Man Made of Words 48.

51. Reichard, Navaho Religion 468.

52. Reichard, Navaho Religion 51.

53. Wyman, Mountainway 67.

54. Reichard, Navaho Religion 408.

55. Bierhorst, Four Masterworks 304.

iii. N. Scott Momaday/The Ancient Child

1. Momaday, Story Teller 124. There exist remarkable similarities between Locke Setman, the novel's protagonist, and N. Scott Momaday. Both are painters, born of Kiowa ancestry in 1934. Therefore, the novel might as well describe a painter's development and could thus be rightly called a 'Künstlerroman'.

2. Momaday, Names foreword. In Kiowa Tales p. xxi, Parsons states that traditional stories start with "There was a camp."

3. "Well, Billy the Kid is a fascinating part of America. He was an outlaw. He . . . was a man who lived to be 21 years old, and in that short time he became a legend on this earth. . . . It's all very fascinating, and, of course, I grew up in the very landscape on which Billy the Kid lived his 21 years. I fantasized as a boy that I rode with Billy the Kid, and what a wonderful thing that was!" (Momaday, Story Teller 124).

4. In Kiowa Voices: Myths, Legends and Folktales 88-93, Kiowa informants told Maurice Boyd the "Bear Lodge Legend" of the "Star Girls." In this version a woman turns into a bear while playing a chase game with her girl friends. She kills all her people with the exception of her younger sister. Aided by hunters the young girl is able to escape from "monster bear" towards a rock which "widened at the base and protruded upward" (92). Together with the young men she climbs the tree up until the sky where she has been staying ever since. In Kiowa Tales, Parsons recounts a similar story called "Star Girl." Again, a woman becomes a bear after her husband had killed the animal, his wife's lover. *Bear Woman* subsequently kills her entire tribe, leaving only one sister and her brothers who had been out hunting. They run away from *Bear Woman* towards a rock which gives them shelter by rising up into the sky. They stay up there until they turn into stars. "The rock still stands leaning over as the Bear Woman left it and with the scratches of Turned-to-Bear upon it" (11).
Although according to traditional Kiowa tales the "person-turned-bear" was a woman and most of the people climbing the rock were men, the Kiowas still refer to the constellation as the "Star Girls" or the "Seven Sisters."

5. Wyman, Mountainway 19.

6. Wyman, Mountainway 17.

7. 'Creator of calamities . . . slanderous and deceitful of gods . . . .' in: Ulf Diederichs, ed., Germanische Götterlehre 249. In her book based on Jungian psychology, Archetypal Patterns in Poetry: Psychological Studies of Imagination 1, Maud Bodkin describes incidents that have happened not to the individual but to his ancestors as "experiences . . . of which the results are inherited in the structure of the brain, *a priori* determinants of individual experience."

8. Momaday, Names foreword. The Hebrew translation of Set, "the appointed," adds further significance to his name.

9. Momaday, Man Made of Words 96.

10. Fr. Berard Haile, "Navaho Chantways and Ceremonials," American Anthropologist 648.

11. Wyman, Mountainway 19.

12. Parsons xv.

13. Frisbie, Navajo Medicine Bundles 2.

14. Reichard, Navaho Religion 406-407.

15. "After some period of time, a child was heard crying for four days. The people could not find the child. They were afraid. First Man finally succeeded in finding a mysterious baby girl. . . . She was Changing Woman." Sheila Moon, Changing Woman and Her Sisters 155.

16. Reichard, Navaho Religion 409.

17. Father Berard Haile, and Mary Wheelwright, Emergence Myth n.p.; in: Moon 169.

18. Parsons 9.

19. Reichard, Navaho Religion 154.

20. Reichard, Navaho Religion 530.

21. Parsons 9; footnote 4.

22. "Some bundles," Reichard explains in Navaho Religion 340, "represent continuous or tribal power, so that when the owner dies, the power . . . held in trust survives."

23. Frisbie, Navajo Medicine Bundles 9.

24. Frisbie, Navajo Medicine Bundles 140.

25. Allen, Sacred Hoop 204-205.

26. Reichard, Navaho Religion 197.

27. Gladys A. Reichard, Navajo Medicine Man 59.

28. Allen, Sacred Hoop 204-205.

29. Wyman, Mountainway 157.

30. Wyman, Mountainway 18-19, 16.

31. Father Berard Haile, Navaho Sacrificial Figurines 4.

32. Wyman, Mountainway 102.

33. Reichard, Navaho Religion 92; comp. also Navaho Religion 384.

34. Wyman, Mountainway 106.

35. Reichard, Navaho Religion 198.

36. Reichard, Navaho Religion 409, 206, 187.

37. Reichard, Navaho Religion 63.

38. Reichard, Navaho Religion 109.

39. Here, the autobiographical relevance of The Ancient Child becomes apparent. As Momaday points out extensively in The Names, Tsoai-talee is the name given him by Pohd-lohk, the storyteller. This storyteller, Momaday writes further, "believed that a man's life proceeds from his name, in the way a river proceeds from its source" (The Names foreword).

40. Allen, Sacred Hoop 243.

41. Reichard, Navaho Religion 413.

42. Wyman, Mountainway 105.

43. Louise Lamphere, "Southwestern Ceremonialism," Handbook of North American Indians 750.

44. Wyman, Mountainway 102.

45. "Die Identität ist hierbei eine keineswegs bloß 'erschlossene', sondern eine mythisch-geglaubte, weil magisch-erlebte und gefühlte Identität". Ernst Cassirer, Philosophie der symbolischen Formen: Das mythische Denken 219.

46. Allen, Sacred Hoop 116-117.

iv. Leslie Marmon Silko/Ceremony

1. Leslie Marmon Silko was born in Albuquerque in 1948. She grew up at Laguna Pueblo. After earning a B.A. in English from the University of New Mexico in 1969, she began law school in a program intended to help Native Americans get their own lawyers, but then gave it up for writing and teaching. She taught creative writing and a course in the oral tradition for the English department at the University of New Mexico. In 1974, she published Laguna Woman, a collection of poems, while several of her prose works were included in Kenneth Rosen's The Man to Send Rain Clouds: Contemporary Stories by American Indians. She taught two years at a Navajo Community College at Tsaile, then spent two years writing Ceremony, in Ketchikan, Alaska, from where she returned to teach at her old university. In 1978 she moved to Tucson to accept a lectureship at the University of Arizona. The Lagunas are a Keresan people whose culture is similar to that of the Jemez Pueblo, the setting of Momaday's House Made of Dawn.

2. Leslie Marmon Silko, Sun Tracks 29-30; as cited in Lincoln, Native American Renaissance 283. Blumenberg stresses the significance of stories when he writes, 'Every story furnishes the institution of bare power with an Achilles' heel'. "Jede Geschichte macht der blanken Macht eine Achillesferse" (22).

3. Allen, Sacred Hoop 119.

4. Elaine Jahner, "An Act of Attention: Event Structure in 'Ceremony,'" Critical Essays on Native American Literature 240.

5. The power of the mythic perspective to shape our experience of the world is also at the heart of Silko's short fiction. In "Yellow Woman," a young Laguna woman meets a Navajo down by the river while she is getting water; when he addresses her as *Yellow Woman*, she begins to wonder whether she is indeed living out a myth. Leslie M. Silko, "Yellow Woman," The Man to Send Rain Clouds: Contemporary Stories by American Indians 33-45.

6. Ruppert 79.

7. Dexter Fisher, interviewer, "Stories and their Tellers - A Conversation with Leslie Marmon Silko," The Third Woman: Minority Women Writers of the United States 19.

8. Reichard, Navaho Religion 65.

9. Lincoln, Native American Renaissance 240.

10. Reichard, Navaho Religion 497.

11. Reichard, Navaho Religion 275.

12. Ruppert 81.

13. Andrew Wiget, Native American Literature 87.

14. Swan 241.

15. While most of the many other interspersed mythic chants are Laguna originals, this one is a little known Keres story. In Keres mythology, the sisters *Naotsete* (later called *Sun Woman*), and *Uretsete* (who later became *Iyatiku*), had problems getting along. Therefore, *Naotsete* decided to go east to create the white race. She said: "We both realize that we will give life to a great many of our own kind, and in a long time from now we shall meet again, and even though much will have changed with us we will still be sisters" (WOS 126).

16. Wyman, Mountainway 8. Reichard, Navaho Religion 656. "Most of the Evil chant myths have an episode relating how the hero was transformed by

Coyote into a mangy coyote, because Coyote, coveting the hero's wife, hit him with a coyote skin. The rite represents the change back to normal." See also Reichard, Navaho Religion 322-323.

17. Wyman, Mountainway 102-103.

18. Wyman, Mountainway 67.

19. Reichard, Navaho Religion 80.

20. Swan 239.

21. The Keres huntress is called *Kochinnenako*, *Yellow Woman*, and her male counterpart, *Arrow Youth*. In some versions of the myth he appears as her husband, in others he functions as her brother. In Keresan mythology, *Kochinnenako*, who is identified with the moon, is the mother of the *Little War Twins*. The *Little War Twins* exist far beyond the confines of the Pueblo world. They clearly resemble their Navajo counterparts, the *War Twins*, in that they matured in a few days and are considered culture heroes. Their father, *Sun*, handed them weapons to save the people from monsters that had been plaguing the human race. Like the Navajo culture heroes, *Monster-Slayer* and *Born-of-Water*, they often need the help of *Spider Woman* who constantly supplies them with advice. In both Keres and Navajo mythology, their impregnation was miraculous: *Kochinnenako* conceived them when one day a ray of *Sun* and a drop of water fell on her while she was asleep.

22. Rosen 35.

23. Tyler, Pueblo Gods and Myths 189.

24. Reichard, Navaho Religion 452. Informants told Boas that Mount Taylor was positioned first by *Spider Woman*, and thus is preeminent among the sacred peaks.

25. Reichard, Navaho Religion 531.

26. Swan 237-238.

27. Haile, Origin Legend of the Navaho Enemy Way 197. Comp. also Reichard, Navaho Religion 207.

28. Allen, Sacred Hoop 226, 123.

29. Boas, Keresan Texts 280; comp. also Stirling 99-108.

30. Susan Blumenthal, "Spotted Cattle and Deer: Spirit Guides and Symbols of Endurance and Healing in 'Ceremony'," American Indian Quarterly 369.

31. Gill, Religious Action 97.

32. Allen, Sacred Hoop 118.

33. Lincoln, Native American Renaissance 249.

34. Reichard, Navaho Religion 149.

35. Paula Gunn Allen, "Yellow Woman Stories," Spider Woman's Granddaughters 210.

36. St. Andrews 86-94.

37. Alfonso Ortiz, "Ritual Drama and the Pueblo World View," New Perspectives on the Pueblos 143.

38. Ruppert 81-82.

v. Paula Gunn Allen/The Woman Who Owned the Shadows

1. Paula Gunn Allen, a Laguna Pueblo/Sioux/Lebanese-American, teaches American Indian Studies at UC Berkeley in San Francisco. An adamant feminist, she wrote The Sacred Hoop. Recovering the Feminine in American Indian Traditions in 1986. Best known as a poet - The Blind Lion (1975), Coyote's Daylight Trip (1978), Star Child (1981), A Cannon Between My Knees (1981), Shadow Country (1982), and Skins and Bones (1988) - The Woman Who Owned the Shadows is her first novel.

2. Allen, The Woman Who Owned the Shadows, dustjacket (back). Since then other such novels, for instance Janet Campbell Hale's The Jailing of Cecilia Capture have been published.

3. Elizabeth Hanson, Forever There: Race and Gender in Contemporary Native American Fiction 57.

4. Allen, Sacred Hoop 109.

5. Carol Pearson and Katherine Pope, The Female Hero in American and British Literature 63.

6. Pearson and Pope, Female Hero 261.

7. 'Ephanie's fall from the apple-tree [is] a symbolic recapitulation of the original sin in Christianity', Zwillus, 186.

8. Mary Daly, Beyond God the Father: Toward a Philosophy of Women's Liberation 67.

9. Allen, Sacred Hoop 48.

10. Pearson and Pope, Female Hero 9.

11. Pearson and Pope, Female Hero 262.

12. Pearson and Pope, Female Hero 262.

13. Tyler, Pueblo Gods and Myths 121, 124.

14. Allen, Sacred Hoop 226.

15. Allen, Sacred Hoop 19.

16. *Ts'its'tsi'nako*'s secular aspect, *Spider Woman*, is a largely benevolent figure who helps people in need. In some instances, however, she can be callous and deceiving, laying her trap for the unsuspecting to get caught. *Spider Woman* appears in the legends of many American Indian cultures, including those of the Navajo. Like most powerful deities, *Spider Woman* has multiple identities, takes on many forms, and has various names. She is *Na'ashę́'ii asdzą́* to the Navajo, and *Kokyang Wuhti* to the Hopi.

17. Bierhorst, The Mythology of North America 1.

18. John Gunn, Schat-Chen: History, Traditions and Narratives of the Queres Indians of Laguna and Acoma 89; as quoted in Pueblo Gods and Myths 91.

19. Allen, Sacred Hoop 100.

20. Allen, Yellow Woman Stories 211.

21. Tyler, Pueblo Gods and Myths 104-105. The remarkable point in all Pueblo emergence accounts is that "only the sisters come out," and that the men "were created below, but do not really come into being until born on the surface of the earth."

22. *Naotsete* and *Uretsete*, for example, are viewed as her coequals who possess the power to vitalize the creatures that inhabit the earth. Similar to *Ts'its'tsi'nako*, they have the ability to "think" creation. Whereas *Ts'its'tsi'nako* used the exclusive power of her imagination, the sister goddesses reached into the basket (bundle) that *Ts'its'tsi'nako* had given them, take out the effigy of the creature, and thought it into life. They are responsible not only for living beings, but for the landscape as well, placing mountains, rivers, and forests.

23. Pearson and Pope, Female Hero 262.

24. In that regard she resembles the Hopi creator-goddess, *Huruing-Wuuti*, *Hard Beings Woman*, who also lived on an island which only later became the earth inhabited by humans. The Hopi consider *Huruing-Wuuti* the Mother of the Universe. As the goddess of hard substances (turquoise, shell, and coral), she is associated with wealth. Old and ugly by day and young and beautiful by night, she is visited daily by *Sun* in her kiva located in the western ocean. Like *Thought Woman*, she did not give birth to creation or to human beings.

In some versions she created by breathing life into male and female effigies that became the parents of the Hopi; in other accounts she created humans by rubbing off "part of her cuticle which is rolled in a ball and hidden under the blanket." The male youth she created is called *Muingwu*, his female counterpart, *Tuwa'bontumsi, Sand Altar Woman. Huruing-Wuuti* is credited most frequently with being the creator of the world, and is said to own the stars and the moon. She is "the mother of the universe, standing coequal with the Sun, and perhaps even more powerful . . . ." In her relationship with *Sun*, her title as "creator of the world," and her ability to change from a young to a mature to an old woman, she resembles *Changing Woman/White Shell Woman* of the Navajo. Tyler links the change from maid to matron to crone to the stages of ripeness in the corn, from green to ripe to harvested corn. Although, as he notes, she is "no mother-of-crops," this comparison would nevertheless establish her clearly as a symbol of fertility (Tyler, Pueblo Gods and Myths 93, 84).

25. The symbol of twins as reflecting duality and/or opposition is wide-spread throughout the Americas irrespective of geography. *Changing Woman* of the Navajo had two sons; *Thought Woman* of the Keres, on the other hand, enlivened two women.

BIBLIOGRAPHY

Primary Sources

Allen, Paula Gunn. The Woman Who Owned the Shadows. San Francisco: Spinster/Aunt Lute, 1983.

---. Skins and Bones. Albuquerque: West End Press, 1988.

Borland, Hal. When the Legends Die. New York: Bantam Books, 1972.

Brown, Dee. Bury My Heart at Wounded Knee. New York: Bantam Books, 1972.

Campbell Hale, Janet. The Jailing of Cecilia Capture. 1985. Albuquerque: University of New Mexico Press, 1987.

Eastman, Charles. Indian Boyhood. 1902. New York: Dover, 1971.

McNickle, D'Arcy. Wind From an Enemy Sky. San Francisco: Harper and Row, 1978.

Momaday, N. Scott. House Made of Dawn. 1966. New York: Harper and Row, 1968.

---. Der Weg zum Regenberg. Trans. Peter Baum. Idstein, Ts.: Baum Publications, 1991.

---. The Way to Rainy Mountain. New York: Ballantine, 1970.

---. The Names: A Memoir. Tucson: The University of Arizona Press, 1976.

---. The Ancient Child. New York: Doubleday, 1989.

Mountain Wolf Woman. "Mountain Wolf Woman." The Portable North American Indian Reader. Ed. Frederick W. Turner III. 1974. New York Penguin Books, 1977. 455-82.

Radin, Paul. "The Autobiography of a Winnebago Indian." The Portable North American Indian Reader. Ed. Frederick W. Turner, III. 1974. New York: Penguin Books, 1977. 378-454.

Silko, Leslie. Ceremony. 1977. New York: Penguin Books, 1988.

---. Storyteller. New York: Seaver, 1981.

---. "Yellow Woman." The Man To Send Rain Clouds: Contemporary Stories by American Indians. Ed. Kenneth Rosen. New York: Random House, 1975. 33-45.

Welch, James. "Snow Country Weavers." South Dakota Review. Summer 1969: 28.

Zitkala-Sa/Gertrude Simmons Bonnin. "The Schooldays of an Indian Girl." Atlantic Monthly Feb. 1900, 185-94.

Secondary Sources

Allen, Paula Gunn. The Sacred Hoop: Recovering the Feminine in American Indian Traditions. Boston: Beacon Press, 1986.

---, ed. Studies in American Indian Literature: Critical Essays and Course Designs. New York: Modern Language Association, 1983.

---. "A Stranger in my Own Life: Alienation in American Indian Prose and Poetry." Melus 7 (1980): 3-19.

---. "'The Grace that Remains' - American Indian Women's Literature." Book Forum 5 (1981): 376-382.

---. "Bringing Home the Fact: Tradition and Continuity in the Imagination." Recovering the Word: Essays on Native American Literature. Ed. Brian Swann and Arnold Krupat. Berkeley: University of California Press, 1987. 563-579.

---, ed. Spider Woman's Granddaughters: Traditional Tales and Contemporary Writing by Native American Women. New York: Ballantine Books, 1989.

---. "Yellow Woman Stories." Spider Woman's Granddaughters. Ed. Paula Gunn Allen. New York: Ballantine Books, 1989. 210-218.

---. "Special Problems in Teaching Leslie Marmon Silko's 'Ceremony." American Indian Quarterly 14.4 (1990): 379-386.

Antell, Judith A. "Momaday, Welch, and Silko: Expressing the Feminine Principle Through Male Alienation." American Indian Quarterly 12.3 (1988): 213-220.

Bahti, Tom. Southwestern Indian Ceremonials. Flagstaff: KC Publications, 1987.

---. Southwestern Indian Tribes. Flagstaff: KC Publications, 1968.

Bartlett, Mary Dougherty. The New Native American Novel: Works in Progress. Albuquerque: University of New Mexico Press, 1986.

Bataille, Gretchen M., and Kathleen Mullen Sands, eds. American Indian Women: Telling Their Lives. Lincoln: University of Nebraska Press, 1984.

Beal, Merrill D. "I Will Fight No More Forever." Chief Joseph And the Nez Perce War. New York: Ballantine, 1963.

Beck, Warren A. New Mexico: A History of Four Centuries. Norman: University of Oklahoma Press, 1962.

Benedict, Ruth. Patterns of Culture. Boston: Houghton Mifflin Company, 1934.

Bevis, William. "Native American Novels: Homing In." Recovering The Word: Essays on Native American Literature. Ed. Brian Swann and Arnold Krupat. Berkeley: University of California Press, 1987. 308-323.

---. "American Indian Verse Translations." Literature of the American Indians: Essays and Interpretations. Ed. Abraham Chapman. New York: New American Library, 1975. 308-323.

Bidney, David. "Myth, Symbolism, and Truth." Myth and Literature: Contemporary Theory and Practice. Ed. John B. Vickery. Lincoln: University of Nebraska Press, 1966.

Bierhorst, John, ed. Four Masterworks of American Indian Literature: Quetzacoatl/The Ritual of Condolence/Cuceb/The Night Chant. New York: Farrar, Strauss, and Giroux, 1974.

---. In the Trail of the Wind: American Indian Poems and Ritual Orations. New York: Farrar, Strauss, and Giroux, 1971.

---. The Mythology of North America. New York: William Morrow Company, 1985.

Black Elk. Black Elk Speaks: Being the Life Story of a Holy Man of the Oglala Sioux. As told through John Neihardt. Lincoln: University of Nebraska Press, 1979.

---. The Sacred Pipe. Ed. Joseph Epes Brown. New York: Penguin Books, 1971.

Blicksilver, Edith. "Traditionalism vs. Modernity: Leslie Silko on American Indian Women." Southwest Review 62 (1979): 149-160.

Blumenthal, Susan. "Spotted Cattle and Deer: Spirit Guides and Symbols of Endurance and Healing in 'Ceremony'." American Indian Quarterly 14.4 (1990): 367-378.

Boas, Franz. Keresan Texts. Publications of the American Ethnological Society 8 (1925-28).

---. Race, Language, and Culture. New York: Free Press, 1940.

Bodkin, Maud. Archetypal Patterns in Poetry: Psychological Studies in Imagination. New York: Vintage Books, 1958.

Bohrer, Karl Heinz. Ed. Mythos und Moderne: Begriff und Bild einer Rekonstruktion. Frankfurt/M.: Suhrkamp, 1983.

Boyd, Maurice. Kiowa Voices: Myths, Legends and Folktales. Fort Worth: Texas Christian University Press, 1983.

Brown, John P. Old Frontiers. Kingsport, Tenn.: State of Wisconsin State Historical Society, Draper Manuscripts, 1938.

Brown, Joseph Epes. The Spiritual Legacy of the American Indian. New York: Crossroad, 1988.

---. See. n.p.: Walter Holden Capps, n.d.

Brumble, H. David, III, and Karl Kroeber. "Reasoning Together." Canadian Review of American Studies 11 (1981): 253-270.

Cahn, Edgar S. Our Brother's Keeper. The Indian in White America. Washington, D.C.: World Publishers, 1969.

Calloway, Colin G., ed. New Directions in American Indian History. Norman: University of Oklahoma Press, 1988.

Campbell, Joseph. The Inner Reaches of Outer Space: Metaphor as Myth and as Religion. New York: A. van der Marck Editions, 1985.

Cassirer, Ernst. Philosophie der symbolischen Formen: Das mythische Denken. 1964. Darmstadt: Wissenschaftliche Buchgesellschaft, 1987.

---. Der Mythus des Staates: Philosophische Grundlagen politischen Verhaltens. 1949. Frankfurt/M.: Fischer, 1988.

Chapman, Abraham, ed. Literature of the American Indian: Views and Interpretations. New York: New American Library, 1975.

Courlander, Harold. Hopi Voices. Albuquerque: University of New Mexico Press, 1982.

Curtis, Edward S. The North American Indian: The Indian of the United States and Alaska. New York: Johnson, 1970.

Daly, Mary. Gyn/Ecology. The Metaethics of Radical Feminism. Boston: Beacon Press, 1978.

Davidson, Cathy N., and E.M. Broner, eds. The Lost Tradition: Mothers and Daughters in Literature. New York: F. Ungar Pub. Co., 1980.

Deloria, Vine Jr. God is Red. New York: Dell Publishing Co., Inc., 1973.

---, ed. Of Utmost Good Faith. 1971. New York: Bantam, 1972.

---. We Talk, You Listen: New Tribes, New Turf. New York: Macmillan, 1970.

Diederichs, Ulf., ed. Germanische Götterlehre. 1984. München: Diederichs, 1989.

Dodson Gray, Elizabeth. Patriarchy as a Conceptual Trap. Wellesley, Mass.: Roundtable Press, 1982.

Dozier, Edward P. The Pueblo Indians of North America. New York: Holt, Rinehart and Winston, Inc., 1968.

Duley, Margot I., and Mary I. Edwards. The Cross-Cultural Study of Women: A Comprehensive Guide. New York: Feminist Press, 1986.

Eggan, Fred. Social Organization of the Western Pueblos. Chicago: University of Chicago Press, 1950.

Eliade, Mircea. Myth and Reality. New York: Harper and Row, 1963.

Espey, David B. "Endings in Contemporary Indian Fiction." Western American Literature 13 (1978): 133-139.

Etienne, Mona, and Eleanor Leacock, eds. Women and Colonization: Anthropological Perspectives. New York Praeger, 1980.

Erdoes, Richard. The Rain Dance People: The Pueblo Indians, Their Past and Present. New York: Alfred Knopf, 1976.

Evers, Lawrence J. "Words and Place: A Reading of 'House Made of Dawn.'" Western American Literature. 11 (1979): 297-320.

Farb, Peter. Man's Rise to Civilization: The Cultural Ascent of the Indians of North America. New York: E.P. Dutton, 1988.

Fiedler, Leslie A., and Houston A. Baker, Jr., eds. English Literature: Opening up the Canon. Baltimore: The Johns Hopkins University Press, 1981.

---. "Literature as an Institution: The View from 1980." English Literature: Opening Up the Canon. Ed. Leslie Fiedler and Houston Baker, Jr. Baltimore: Johns Hopkins University Press, 1981.

---. The Return of the Vanishing American. New York: Stein and Day, 1969.

Fischer, Dexter. The Third Woman: Minority Women Writers of the United States. Boston: Houghton Mifflin Co., 1980.

---. "Stories and Their Tellers - A Conversation With Leslie Marmon Silko." The Third Woman: Minority Women Writers of the United States. Boston: Houghton Mifflin Co., 1980.

Ford, Richard I., and Albert H. Schroeder, and Stewart L. Peckham. "Three Perspectives on Puebloan Prehistory." New Perspectives on the Pueblos. Ed. Alfonso Ortiz. Albuquerque: University of New Mexico Press, 1972. 19-39.

Foreman, Carolyn. Indian Women Chiefs. Washington, D.C.: Zenger Publishing Co., 1976.

Frisbie, Charlotte J., ed. Southwestern Indian Ritual Drama. Albuquerque: University of New Mexico Press, 1980.

---. Navajo Medicine Bundles or **Jish**: Acquisition, Transmission, and the Disposition in the Past and Present. Albuquerque: University of New Mexico Press, 1987.

Frye, Northrop. "The Archetypes of Literature." Criticism: The Major Statements. Ed. Charles Kaplan. New York: St. Martin's Press, 1975. 547-561.

---. "The Koine of Myth." Myth and Metaphor: Selected Essays, 1974-1988. Ed. Robert D. Denham. Charlottesville: University of Virginia Press, 1990. 3-17.

Gill, Sam D. Mother Earth: An American Story. Chicago: The University of Chicago Press, 1987.

---. Native American Religious Action: A Performance Approach to Religion. Columbia, SC: University of South Carolina Press, 1987.

---. Native American Traditions: Sources and Interpretations. Belmont, CA: Wadsworth Pub. Co., 1983.

---. Sacred Words: A Study of Navajo Religion and Prayer. Wesport: Greenwood Press, 1981.

---. "Navajo Views of Their Origin." Handbook of North American Indians. Ed. Alfonso Ortiz. Vol. 10. Washington: Smithsonian Institute, 1983. 502-505.

Gorman, Carl N. "Navajo Vision of Earth and Man." The Indian Historian 6.1 (1973): 17-23.

Gunn, John M. Schat-Chen: History, Traditions and Narratives of the Queres Indians of Laguna and Acoma. Albuquerque: Albright and Anderson, 1917.

Habermas, Jürgen. "Die Verschlingung von Mythos und Aufklärung: Bemerkungen zur *Dialektik der Aufklärung* - nach einer erneuten Lektüre." Mythos und Moderne: Begriff und Bild einer Rekonstruktion. Ed. Karl Heinz Bohrer. Frankfurt/M.: Suhrkamp, 1983. 405-431.

Hackett, C.W., and C.C. Shelby. Revolt of the Pueblo Indians of New Mexico and Otermin's Attempted Reconquest, 1680-1682. Coronado Historical Series, Vols. 3, 8 and 9: Albuquerque University of New Mexico Press, 1942.

Haile, Berard. Origin Legend of the Navaho Enemy Way. New Haven: Yale University Press, 1938.

---. "Navaho Chantways and Ceremonials." American Anthropologist. 40 (1938): 639-652.

---. Navaho Sacrificial Figurines. Chicago (n.p.) 1947.

---, trans. "The Myth of Beautyway." Beautyway: A Navaho Ceremonial. Ed. Leland C. Wyman. New York: Pantheon Books, 1957.

---. "Rules Laid Down for Beautyway." Ed. Leland C. Wyman. Beautyway: A Navaho Ceremonial. New York: Bollingen Series LIII - Pantheon Books, 1957.

---, and Mary Wheelwright. Emergence Myth. Santa Fe, NM: Museum of Navajo Ceremonial Art, Inc., 1949.

---. Starlore Among the Navaho. Santa Fe: Museum of Navajo Ceremonial Art, 1974.

Hanson, Elizabeth I. Forever There: Race and Gender in Contemporary Native American Fiction. New York: Peter Lang Publishing, Inc., 1989.

Harvey, David. Closing General Session. Deutsche Gesellschaft für Amerikastudien, Berlin. 12 June, 1992.

Hawley, Florence. "Pueblo Social Organization As a Lead to Pueblo History." American Anthropologist 39 (n.d.) 504-522.

Heinerman, John. Spiritual Wisdom of the Native Americans. San Rafael, CA: Cassandra Press, 1989.

Hester, James J. Navajo Migrations and Acculturation. Albuquerque: University of New Mexico Press, 1962.

Highwater, Jamake. The Primal Mind: Vision and Reality in Indian America. New York: New American Library, 1981.

Hobson, Geary. The Remembered Earth: An Anthology of Native American Literature. Albuquerque: Red Earth Press, 1979.

Hogan, Linda. "Who Puts Together." Studies in American Indian Literature: Critical Essays and Course Designs. New York: MLA, 1983. 169-177.

Hymes, Dell. "In Vain I Tried to Tell You": Essays in Native American Ethnopoetics. Philadelphia: University of Pennsylvania Press, 1981.

Jackson, Donald, ed. Black Hawk: An Autobiography. Urbana: University of Illinois Press, 1964.

Jahner, Elaine. "An Act of Attention: Event Structure in 'Ceremony.'" Critical Essays on Native American Literature. Boston: C.G. Hall & Co., 1985. 211-224.

Jay, Gregory S. "The End of 'American' Literature: Toward a Multicultural Practice." College English 53. 3 (1991): 264-280.

Jennings, Francis. The Invasion of America. Indians, Colonialism, and the Cant of Conquest. Chapel Hill: University of North Carolina Press, 1975.

Kaplan, Charles, ed. Criticism: The Major Statements. New York: St. Martin's Press, 1975.

Katz, Jane B., ed. "Leslie Silko, Laguna Poet and Novelist." This Song Remembers: Self-Portraits of Native Americans in the Arts. Boston: Houghton Mifflin, 1980.

Kemper, Peter. Ed. Macht des Mythos - Ohnmacht der Vernunft? Frankfurt/M.: Fischer, 1989.

Klah, Hasteen. Navajo Creation Myths: The Story of the Emergence. Recorded by Mary C. Wheelwright. 1942. Santa Fe: Museum of Navajo Ceremonial Art, 1980.

Kluckhohn, Clyde, and Dorothea Leighton. The Navajo. Cambridge: The Harvard University Press, 1946.

Kroeber, Karl, ed. Studies in American Indian Literature. 9.1 (1985): 1-41.

---. Traditional Literature of the American Indian: Text and Interpretations. Lincoln: University of Nebraska Press, 1981.

Krupat, Arnold. For Those Who Come After: A Study of Native American Autobiography. Berkeley: University of California Press, 1985.

---. "Identity and Difference in the Criticism of Native American Literature." Diacritics 13 (1983): 2-13.

Kuper, Adam. The Invention of Primitive Society: Transformations of an Illusion. London: Routledge, 1988.

Lame Deer, John (Fire) (Lakota), and Richard Erdoes. Lame Deer: Seeker of Visions. The Life of a Sioux Medicine Man. New York: Simon and Schuster, 1972.

Lamphere, Louise. "Symbolic Elements in Navajo Ritual." Southwestern Journal of Anthropology 25 (1969): 279-305.

---. "Southwestern Ceremonialism." Handbook of North American Indians. Alfonso Ortiz, ed. Washington: Smithsonian Institute, 1983. 743-763.

Larson, Charles R. American Indian Fiction. Albuquerque: University of New Mexico Press, 1978.

Lauter, Paul. "The Literatures of America: A Comparative Discipline." Redefining American Literary History. Eds. A LaVonne Brown Ruoff, and Jerry M. Ward. New York: MLA, 1990. 9-34.

Lévi-Strauss, Claude. Mythos und Bedeutung. Frankfurt/M.: Suhrkamp, 1980.

Lincoln, Kenneth. Native American Renaissance. Berkeley: University o f California Press, 1983.

Lindig, Wolfgang, and Mark Muentzel. Die Indianer. München: Deutscher Taschenbuch Verlag, 1978.

Luckert, Karl W. The Navajo Hunter Tradition. Tucson: University of Arizona Press, 1975.

---. Navajo Mountain and Rainbow Bridge Religion. Flagstaff: Museum of Northern Arizona, 1977.

---. Coyoteway: A Navajo Holyway Healing Ceremonial. Flagstaff: Museum of Northern Arizona Press, 1979.

---. A Navajo Holyway Healing Ceremonial. Tucson: The University of Arizona Press,1979. Malinowski, Bronislaw. "Myth in Primitive Psychology." Magic, Science, Religion, and Other Essays. Boston: Free Press, 1948. 72-88.

Matthews, Washington. "Navaho Myths, Prayers, And Songs With Texts And Translations." American Archaeology And Ethnology. Ed. Putnam, Frederick, and A. L. Kroeber. Berkeley: The University Press, 1907-1910. 21-63.

---, trans. Navaho Legends. 1897. New York: Kraus Reprint Co., 1969.

McNeley, James Kale. Holy Wind in Navajo Philosophy. Tucson: University of Arizona Press, 1981.

McNickle, D'Arcy. Native American Tribalism: Indian Survivals and Renewals. 1973. New York: Oxford Press, 1979.

Momaday, N. Scott. Interview. "Story Teller." The Journal of Ethnic Studies 16.1 (1986): 118-126.

---. "The Man Made of Words." Literature of the American Indian: Views and Interpretations. Ed. Abraham Chapman. New York: New American Library, 1975. 96-110.

Moon, Sheila. Changing Woman and her Sisters. San Francisco: Guild for Psychological Studies, 1984.

Mullet, G.M. Spider Woman Stories: Legends of the Hopi Indians. Tucson: University of Oklahoma Press, 1979.

Nabokov, Peter, ed. Native American Testimony: An Anthology of Indian and White Relations: First Encounter to Dispossession. New York: Harper and Row, 1978.

---. "American Indian Literature: A Tradition of Renewal." ASAIL Newsletter 2 (1978): 37.

Nicholson, Shirley, ed. The Goddess Re-Awakening: The Feminine Principle Today. Wheaton, Ill.: The Theosophical Publishing House, 1989.

Olson, Carl, ed. The Book of the Goddess. Past and Present. New York: Crossroad, 1989.

Ortiz, Alfonso. "Ritual Drama and the Pueblo World View." New Perspectives on the Pueblos. Ed. Alfonso Ortiz. Albuquerque: University of New Mexico Press, 1972. 135-161.

---, ed. Handbook of North American Indians. Vol. 9. Washington: Smithsonian Institute, 1979.

---, ed. Handbook of North American Indians. Vol 10. Washington: Smithsonian Institute, 1983.

Parsons, Elsie Clews. Kiowa Tales. 1929. New York: Kraus Reprint Co., 1969.

Pearson, Carol, and Katherine Pope. The Female Hero in American and British Literature. New York: Bowker, 1981.

Powers, Marla N. Oglala Women: Myth, Ritual and Reality. Chicago: University of Chicago Press, 1986.

Prucha, Francis Paul, S.J., ed. Americanizing the American Indian: Writing by the "Friends of the Indians," 1800-1900. Cambridge: Harvard University Press, 1973.

Raines, Howell. "American Indians Struggling for Power and Identity." New York Times Magazine 11 Feb. 1979.

Ramsey, Jarold. Reading the Fire: Essays in the Traditional Indian Literatures of the Far West. Lincoln: University of Nebraska Press, 1983.

Rank, Otto. The Myth of the Birth of the Hero. New York: Vintage Books, 1959.

Reichard, Gladys A. Navajo Medicine Man. New York: J.J. Augustin, 1939.

---. Social Life of the Navajo Indians. New York: Columbia University Press, 1928.

---. Navaho Religion. A Study of Symbolism. Princeton, N.J.: Bollingen Series XVIII-Princeton University Press, 1970.

Rose, Wendy. "American Indian Poets - and Publishing." Book Forum. Ed. Elaine Jahner 4.3 (1981): 402.

Rosen, Kenneth, ed. The Man to Send Rain Clouds. Contemporary Stories by American Indians. New York: Vintage Books, 1975.

Ruoff, A. LaVonne Brown. "American Indian Literatures: A Guide to Anthologies, Texts, and Research." Studies in American Indian Literature: Critical Essays and Course Designs. Ed. Paula Gunn Allen. New York: MLA, 1983. 281-310.

---, and Jerry Ward, Jr., eds. Redefining American Literary History. New York: MLA, 1990.

Ruppert, James. "The Reader's Lesson in 'Ceremony.'" Arizona Quarterly 44.1 (1988): 78-85.

Sanday, Peggy Reeves. Female Power and Male Dominance: On the Origins of Sexual Inequality. Cambridge, NY: University of Cambridge Press, 1981.

Sanders, T.E., and Walter W. Peek. Literature of the American Indian. Beverly Hills: Glencoe Press, 1976.

Sando, Joe S. The Pueblo Indians. Albuquerque: The Indian Historian Press, 1976.

Scholes, France V. "Civil Government and Society in the Seventeenth Century." Mexico Historical Review 10 (n.d.) 71-111.

Schubnell, Matthias. N. Scott Momaday: The Cultural and Literary Background. Norman: The University of Oklahoma Press, 1985.

Seyersted, Per. Leslie Marmon Silko. Boise: Boise State University Press, 1980.

Shirer Mathes, Valerie. "A New Look at the Woman in Indian Society." American Indian Quarterly 2.2 (1975): 131-139.

Silko, Leslie Marmon. "Language and Literature from a Pueblo Indian Perspective." Ed. Leslie Fiedler and Houston Baker, Jr. English Literature: Opening Up the Canon. Baltimore: The Johns Hopkins University Press, 1981. 54-72.

---. Interview. Sun Tracks. n.p. n.p. n.d.

Spicer, Edward H. Perspectives in American Indian Culture Change. Chicago: University of Chicago Press, 1961.

St. Andrews, B.A. "Healing the Witchery: Medicine in Silko's 'Ceremony.' "Arizona Quarterly 44.1 (1988) 86-94.

Steiner, Stan. The New Indians. New York: Dell Delta Books, 1968.

Stephen, A. M. Hopi Journal. New York: Columbia University Press, 1936.

Stirling, Matthew W. Origin Myth Of Acoma And Other Records. Washington: United States Government Printing Office, 1942.

Stone, Merlin. When God was a Woman. New York: Dial Press, 1976.

---. Ancient Mirrors of Womanhood. 1979. Boston: Beacon Press, 1984.

Swan, Edith. "Laguna Symbolic Geography and Silko's 'Ceremony.'"American Indian Quarterly 12.3 (1988): 229-249.

Swann, Brian, ed. Smoothing the Ground. Essays on Native American Oral Literature. Berkeley: University of California Press, 1983.

---, and Arnold Krupat, eds. I Tell You Now: Autobiographical Essays by Native American Writers. Lincoln: University of Nebraska Press, 1987.

---. Recovering the Word. Essays on Native American Literature. Berkeley: University of California Press, 1987.

Tedlock, Dennis. Finding the Center. New York: Dial, 1972.

---. "Pueblo Literature: Style and Verisimilitude." New Perspectives on the Pueblos. Ed. Alfonso Ortiz. Albuquerque: University of New Mexico Press, 1972.

---. The Spoken Word and the Work of Interpretation. Philadelphia: University of Pennsylvania Press, 1983.

---, and Barbara Tedlock. Teachings from the American Earth: Indian Religion and Philosophy. New York: n.p., 1975.

Thompson, Laura. "Logico-Aesthetic Integration in Hopi Culture." American Anthropologist 47 (1945): 540-553.

Turner, Frederick W. III, ed. The Portable North American Indian Reader. 1974. New York: Penguin Books, 1977.

Tyler, Hamilton A. Pueblo Gods and Myths. Norman: University of Oklahoma Press, 1964.

---. Pueblo Animals and Myths. Norman: University of Oklahoma Press, 1975.

Velie, Alan. Four American Indian Literary Masters: Scott Momaday, James Welch, Leslie Marmon Silko, and Gerald Vizenor. Norman: University of Oklahoma Press, 1982.

Waters, Frank. Masked Gods: Navajo and Pueblo Ceremonialism. 1950. New York: Ballantine Books, 1970.

---. The Book of the Hopi. 1963. New York: Penguin Books, 1977.

Weigle, Marta. Spiders and Spinsters: Women and Mythology. Albuquerque: University of New Mexico Press, 1982.

Weiler, Dagmar. "N. Scott Momaday: Storyteller." Journal of Ethnic Studies 16.1 (1988): 118-126.

Welch, Deborah. "American Indian Women: Reaching Beyond the Myth." New Directions in American Indian History. Ed. Colin G. Calloway. Norman: University of Oklahoma Press, 1988. 31-48.

Wheeler-Vogelin, Erminie, and R.W. Moore. "The Emergence Myth in Native America." Indiana University Publications in Folklore 9 (1957): 66-91.

Wiget, Andrew. Native American Literature. Boston: Twayne Publishers, 1985.

Witherspoon, Gary. Language and Art in the Navajo Universe. Ann Arbor: University of Michigan Press, 1977.

Woodard, Charles, ed. Ancestral Voice: Conversations with N. Scott Momaday. Lincoln: University of Nebraska Press, 1989.

Wyman, Leland C., ed. Beautyway: A Navajo Ceremonial. New York: Bollingen Series LIII-Pantheon Books, 1957.

---. The Mountainway of the Navajo. Tucson, AZ: The University of Arizona Press, 1975.

---. "Navajo Ceremonial System." Handbook of North American Indians. Alfonso Ortiz, ed. Vol. 10. Washington: Smithsonian Institute, 1983. 536-557.

Ywahoo, Dhyani. Voices of Our Ancestors: Cherokee Teachings from the Wisdom Fire. Boston: Shambhala, 1987.

Zolbrod, Paul G. "Poetry and Culture: The Navajo Example." Ed. Brian Swann. Smoothing the Ground. Essays on Native American Oral Literature. Berkeley: University of California Press, 1983.

---. Dine bahane': The Navajo Creation Story. Albuquerque: The University of New Mexico Press, 1984.

---. "When Artifacts Speak, What Can They Tell Us?" Recovering the Word: Essays on Native American Literature. Ed. Brian Swann and Arnold Krupat. Berkeley: University of California Press, 1987. 13-40.

Zwillus, Frauke. Today's Talk in Yesterday's Voice. Frankfurt/M: Peter Lang Verlag, 1989.